MW00655623

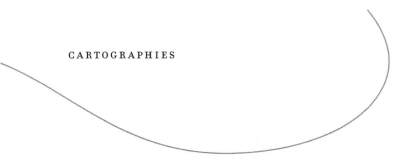

CARTOGRAPHIES

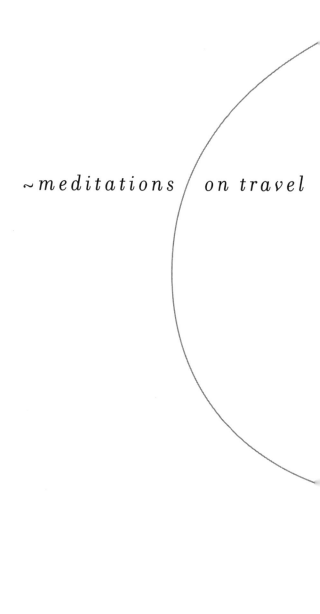

~meditations on travel

BY MARJORIE AGOSÍN

cartographies

Translated and with

an Introduction

by Nancy Abraham Hall

Prelude by Isabel Allende

The University of Georgia Press

Athens and London

Published by the University of Georgia Press

Athens, Georgia 30602

© 2004 by Marjorie Agosín

All rights reserved

Designed by Mindy Basinger Hill

Set in 10.5/15 Filosofia

Printed and bound by Maple-Vail

The paper in this book meets the guidelines for

permanence and durability of the Committee on

Production Guidelines for Book Longevity of the

Council on Library Resources.

Printed in the United States of America

08   07   06   05   04   c   5   4   3   2   1

Library of Congress Cataloging-in-Publication Data

Agosín, Marjorie.

Cartographies : meditations on travel / by Marjorie Agosín ;

translated and with an introduction by Nancy Abraham Hall ;

prelude by Isabel Allende.

p. cm.

ISBN 0-8203-2629-1 (hardcover : alk. paper)

1. Voyages and travels. 2. Agosín, Marjorie—Travel. I. Title.

G465.A37 2004

910.4—dc22   2004001357

British Library Cataloging-in-Publication Data available

contents

prelude

The reader will find in these cartographies a place to dream
and to recuperate an internal compass. Travel, in these
meditations, becomes an audacious adventure, a journey of
memory and the imagination.

With luminosity, passion, and lyrical prose, *Cartographies*
allows the reader to explore cities, sites of imagination,
landscapes of the soul. *Cartographies* is a book to savor, to read
slowly.

Marjorie Agosín's poetic language engages the reader in a
mesmerizing journey of inward reflection. With these prose
poems as our guide, we traverse history's darkest places yet
are reminded of the endurance of the human spirit.

~ ISABEL ALLENDE

introduction

As in life, travelers in literature are propelled by any
number of motives: a sacred quest, a call to arms, a thirst
for adventure. They dream of freedom, pursue economic
gain, yearn for home, or seek redemption on the road.
Some aspire to defend the weak, conquer the other, or
simply describe the endless variety of people and places
they encounter. The earliest known epic poem, written in
the Akkadian language and originating in Mesopotamia
in the third millennium B.C., tells the story of Gilgamesh,
a semi-divine hero who leaves home to find the secret of
eternal life. Greek literature opens with the adventures of
Odysseus and his friends, whose journey home to Ithaca
following the Trojan War lasts for years. And when the
imprisoned Venetian explorer Marco Polo pens an account
of his overland journey to China, he creates the text that
inspires Christopher Columbus to search for a sea passage
to the East. In Spain the modern novel is born the moment
Don Quixote and Sancho sally forth from their corner

of La Mancha, and the New World acquires shape thanks to the observant gazes and inspired visions of a host of real and imagined travelers: Bernal Díaz del Castillo, Alexander von Humboldt, Huckleberry Finn, Jack Kerouac.

Contemporary Latin American literature is filled with imaginative tales of journeys. Strong and unforgettable voices take us up steep mountains crowned by ancient ruins (Neruda's *Canto General*) and down into rural valleys populated by the living dead (Rulfo's *Pedro Páramo*). As readers we travel deep into the rain forest to encounter the origins of music (Carpentier's *Los pasos perdidos*) and out onto an open plain to face a violent yet ideal end (Borges's "El sur"). In Cortázar's *Rayuela*, Horacio Oliveira's life shifts back and forth between Buenos Aires and Paris, while bands of gypsies wander with similar unpredictability in and out of García Márquez's mythical Macondo *(Cien años de soledad).* More recently, women writers have begun to craft journeys of their own, exploring a wide variety of old and new forms of travel. Ana Lydia Vega's barely seaworthy boat full of refugees leaves the Caribbean for U.S. shores ("Encancaranublado") while Carmen Boullosa's young and traumatized protagonist jets from Mexico to London, then on to Germany in search of her father and an adult life as a scholar and writer *(Treinta años).*

With *Cartographies*, poet and award-winning human rights activist Marjorie Agosín joins her unique voice to the community of literature's bold and inspired travelers. In this luminous book Agosín returns to the autobiographical mode of

The Alphabet in My Hands to evoke the many cities, towns, and villages on four continents she has visited or called home. Divided into seven sections, *Cartographies* opens with "A Map of My Face," a series of short pieces designed to introduce and define the voice that will guide the reader on this deeply felt and very personal journey. Dispelling any pretense of objectivity, the first-person narrator eschews causality and logic as she surrenders to the hypnotic rhythm of the heart and the mysterious flow of dreams. Aware that she must make the journey alone, she nevertheless gains strength from her parents, husband, books, amulets, and signs that help her to be fearless, to take her time and resist the urge to control, to trust her own body and instincts. Fortified yet open, she sets out to decipher the ambiguous, secret map of her memory, which "does not betray."

The journey begins along "Southern Shores" as Agosín revisits Chile, the country where she spent her childhood and which she was forced to leave at fourteen when her father, a distinguished professor of chemistry, accepted a teaching post in the United States. The family's departure from Chile coincided with Salvador Allende's election to the presidency and his eventual removal from power by General Augusto Pinochet in 1973. Marjorie's peers bore the brunt of the violence that followed, as traditionally democratic and stable Chile was gripped by a brutal right-wing repression in which thousands of people were "disappeared." The traveler returns to Chile to speak out about what happened there:

I wanted to dream about my country, draw near to her as if for the first time, with the innocence of the little girl who asks where they put the dead people. My country was a sharp desert where women rested upon a silenced history. . . . I wanted to know that long and narrow piece of land, to traverse her body like that of a young woman who has yet to bear children. It was then that I came upon the brutal beauty and horror of the poppy fields.

The women of Chile claim the traveler's attention in a special way as she sees in their work, and especially their creative endeavors, a deep vein of hope and love that runs counter to the hatred and violence at the surface of Chile's recent political life. The potters of Pomaire and the wool makers of Isla Negra are two of these remarkable communities: "We visited the silent and small women who tell their stories through wool. They embroider landscapes, the harvest, the sowing, the May cross—life amid the colored waters. We visited people we loved and the landscapes they created."

If Chile's capital, Santiago, is remembered as the city where "I learned to read Hebrew and Spanish, where I recited the Lord's Prayer," other cities lay special claim to the narrator's memory as well. The northern seaport of Valparaíso, a mischievous place of "magical hills, fish, and poverty," is home to five important figures: her grandparents and great-grandparents Marcos, Josefina, Helena, and Joseph, and Pablo Neruda, Chile's greatest poet, who built

a house in the clouds overlooking the city that received her
forebears as they fled the Holocaust. The blue and startling
lights that dot the hills above Valparaíso "gesture like small
lanterns offering the most generous of gifts." They tell stories
in which the traveler is able to see her own reflection "as
in a mirror devoured by the insistence of memory," and in
particular, the story of Helena Broder's crossing into exile.
In the passage titled "The City of Foreigners," it is not clear
whether "she" is Helena leaving Europe for South America or
Marjorie leaving Chile to live in the United States:

> When she had to leave her country suddenly, she
> remembered its infinite horizon and felt the dawn in her
> hands. She did not know whether her eyes could contain
> the size of the sea or her tears. No one was able to recognize
> her. . . . She learned to accept her destiny, that of a foreign
> woman. . . .

The image of beloved family members reaching southern
shores "on phantom ships" prompts the traveler to retrace
their steps and explore Europe. "Cities of War" opens in
Prague, home to her cousins Tamara and Silvia Broder, who
perished at the hands of the Nazis. There Marjorie Agosín
accompanies her parents to the Pinkas Synagogue, the first of
many stops at Jewish landmarks on her European itinerary.
Each visit becomes a profoundly moving experience for
the traveler, her companions, and ultimately the reader.
Following an outing to the nearby concentration camp, the
narrator observes: "We return to Prague moist with the ovens'

vapors, fearful in the knowledge that the sun has forsaken Terezin. We return, and there is Prague—noble, radiant, and dreamy—and only we have changed." In Vienna and Budapest, too, ghosts of the Holocaust slip in and out of view as the narrator intuits the layers of persecution and injustice that have been part of those cities' histories. And when we travel southward towards Dubrovnik and Sarajevo, present-day suffering comes into focus against a background of ancient hatreds.

The fourth section of *Cartographies*, "Gestures of Memory," begins in Greece, where we meet Julia, the caretaker of the synagogue at Rhodes. Like the poet herself, who is at once fully grown and a child, Julia is described as an "ancient young woman, as small as a thimble, like a dream full of clouds." This astonishing figure is also a writer, for she inscribes "the sadness of her stories on the grotto-like stones, assuring me that truth could be found only in the traces of the wind. . . ." One of these strong breezes propels the traveler and her companions across the Aegean Sea to Istanbul, Jerusalem, and finally Cairo, where the narrator can hear corpses cry out from their graves in the City of the Dead. The voices of the victims of injustice are just as audible in Cairo as they were in Terezin and the poppy fields of Chile, and the mission of the traveler is to bear witness:

> Poetry is no more than this, a passion for telling. Poetry is a gesture of memory intended to cover absence, an extension of the truth. Poetry requires that they be named and found.

Poetry demands to know the whereabouts of oblivion. I
write in order to survive. I become their words and my own.
There is little distance between the living and the dead, and
I choose life.

After Cairo, the path winds back to Europe, this time via
Italy. Although the traveler continues to see and remember
the spirits of the persecuted, in section five, "Touching the
Sky," she is also refreshed and soothed by fountains and
landscape. Moving northward from Malta towards Venice,
than west to Iberia, she delights in once again hearing the
sounds of the Spanish language: "I heard the song, the
closeness of the syllables, the pauses between vowels, and
a fire beyond memory and skin." While she remembers
the terrible fate of the Jews of Toledo, she also stresses that
travelers like Robert Graves, Frédéric Chopin, and George
Sand lived in the villages that she, too, visits. Above all, she
recalls that another Jewish woman, Saint Teresa of Ávila, was
able to write in Spain with language "like slippery grains of
sand, transforming itself, changing color and texture like a
voice done and undone":

> Teresa of Ávila, you walk through your city to the beat of the
> landscape, small ashes clinging to your hair, your face a wide
> mouthful of light. . . . We walk along the walls of Ávila, but
> for you neither time nor walls exist. There are no nations
> or borders. All that exists is the task called word, prayer, or
> faithful presence within your language.

More borders are traversed in "Northern Realms" as the narrator visits Ireland, England, Denmark, Germany, Poland, and Russia. Here, too, she finds herself, Chile, and the fate of the Jewish people reflected in the people and their landscapes: "Why did we go to Ireland? . . . Perhaps I went . . . to reconstruct the story of my own country, with its many broken dreams, its clouded history, [or] because it made me think of women . . . scattered by a diaspora, real or imagined." The nightmare of her family's past is again touched upon in "Amsterdam and Anne Frank" and "There," while the composer Jean Sibelius and poet Anna Akhmatova are among those individuals honored as heroes. In particular, Agosín admires the aristocratic Russian for her language ("a beacon that interrogates and illuminates every homecoming") as well as the deep compassion that informs her work:

> And there you are, Anna, beautiful, intrepid, irresistibly brave. And when you recite a poem, the captive city opens up. . . . All the nameless heroes appear, the defeated Jews, the women with their rose-colored baskets of hunger . . .

Like Akhmatova, Marjorie Agosín wishes to validate and pay homage to the lives of women on the margins of society. "Northern Realms" closes with a tribute to a particular group of "unreachable and disconnected . . . alienated and perverse" women with whom she strongly identifies:

> The gypsy women of Saint Petersburg slumber on the rivers above the palaces of floating mirrors. I approach them and ask

about their daring and audacious travels. As I bid them farewell,
I recognize that their lives are those of women in perpetual
flight, always in darkness, always alone, as if in pain, as
if translucent. . . .

The gypsies of Saint Petersburg find an echo halfway around
the world in another community of extraordinary women,
the basket weavers of Charleston, North Carolina. Descended
from slaves, these "proud and rebellious, always noble"
women "testify about history and its painful secrets" as they
turn straw into baskets, "grateful for the bread that rests
within them, the mute centuries, the dreams betrayed."
Agosín's tribute to these women opens the final section of
Cartographies, titled simply "America," in which the traveler
moves north to south down the entire continent—through
North Carolina, Florida, Texas, New Mexico, Mexico, Central
America, the Caribbean, Brazil, and Uruguay, where painful
memories of youthful exile are rekindled. The journey
then shifts back to the United States, passing through four
locations that have exercised a profound influence on her
life and those she most deeply loves: Georgia, Illinois,
Massachusetts, and finally coastal Maine.

The fog that embroiders the roads along New England's
northernmost shores is not unlike the mists Marjorie Agosín
knew as a girl in Chile. And it is in Ogunquit, Maine, that
the poet is able to find peace in the small summer house so
reminiscent of the stone cottage of her childhood summers
in Isla Negra. From her new home on the cliffs of Maine,

the poet assures us that travelers surprised by fog are indeed
fortunate, for they are likely to discover "the scratched and
oblique light of the eternal horizon, and the beginning of
memory, which is the first journey." As *Cartographies* comes
to a close, the poet urges her readers to "allow the fog to grab
[you] by the waist and sweep [you] into the clear darkness of
the pine groves, entering the forest without hostility . . . be
subtle, like a shaft of light or a mirage along the road."

~ NANCY ABRAHAM HALL
Wellesley College

~ a map of my face

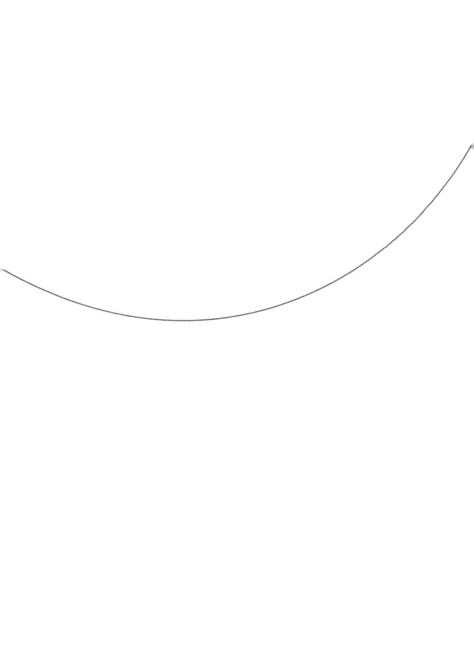

creating a map

I navigated without maps or precise schedules. I intuited that
genuine cartography is hidden, invisible to hours and routes.
I allowed myself to be swept along as if my body were blank.
I eschewed directions and travel times. I understood that no
one awaits a true traveler, that I was alone. Day and night were
contained within me. I looked at my hands and understood
heredity. I understood how the rhythm of a heart devoid of
armor creates a map, imprecise yet full of remembrance and
discoveries, like entering a secret.

the murmur of the road

And I know that I will find neither offerings nor promises. All
that matters is listening to the murmur of the road, following
the route, ignoring other tracks, traveling as if only one possible path existed: the present.

promises

And I travel by choice and by chance in order to recover
a fragrance or perhaps to honor the memory of someone
who asks me to visit a certain place, this island or that cemetery wrapped in mist. And the places call upon me to fulfill

promises, and my feet, free of reason's watchful eye, dance upon the earth, invited by the splendor of all journeys and the marvels of every trail.

a compass and a purple sailboat

I surrounded myself with tiny objects that reminded me of certain cities: a purple sailboat, an erratic compass, an imaginary talisman, and a heart left in the shadows.

the city of memory

In order to draw near to the City of Memory, I must exercise caution and accept both the ambiguity and the clear texture of the place. I must let the city rest peacefully, undisturbed by the resurgence of haste. Memory does not betray, and no matter how often denied, it suddenly appears like a veiled woman, cloudlike and solitary, searching for a word that will name her and find her. In the cities of memory, I must choose unhurried time, the seasons of light, and allow myself to be swept away by origins.

I searched in vain. At the end of the day, and despite all my efforts, I failed to return to the blue house or the patio where I took my first steps. No remnant of the house remained standing, only the cobwebs besieged by a ribbon of smoke. I wanted to find the ship that had taken me to the other side

and the wise old women who blessed my crossing before it
began. I found only the defoliated skin of death. I understood
there would be no way to return to my country. I belonged to
a population condemned to vagrancy, to exile, and to home-
comings that take place only in dreams.

the city of books

I entered the City of Books, dark jewels hoarded in temples
and cathedrals. In this city I found buried candelabra and
stories waiting to be read during nights of sea and moon.
I loved the City of Books where lost gazelles wandered in
search of signs. Like a cabalist, I searched for signs in order
to invent myself through memory. And I read, insensible to
my lips, surrounded by dolls, my hands placed passionately
upon the letters, my voice like a river. That's how I reached
the City of Books. By caressing their spines and edges, I re-
claimed the beauty of their hard covers. Each letter emanated
a story, each story was a secret and clairvoyant letter.

the city of love

Last night I wanted to make of your body a city. I was not cautious. I lost myself in the fire of your face that in my hands became clear like a sacred flame. In the deepest recesses and at
the moment of joy, when your mouth was a harbor or a never

distant beacon, I told myself that the City of Love is like a body awaiting surrender, a body yearning for another without haste, exhaling day and night, light and darkness. Two people making love, the astonishment released by entwined arms, a tongue suspended like a drawbridge above another. Then I told myself that I had arrived at the City of Love, walking slowly, with the gentle beating of beloved objects that appear on the riverbanks of dreams.

a map of my face

Little by little I discovered that my face was a fragile, dangerous, and enigmatic map. Each wrinkle pointed toward a clear and dark destiny. I learned to count the crevices in my skin as a person tallies loves, those required and not. I paused to consider each one, some like expanding cypresses, others like small boats adrift on the sea. Wise men will tell you that the face is a map of the soul. Such ancient men believe that growing old is the greatest possible honor, as only from the depths of one's soul can a heart take shape, like a pitcher of water, a magic vessel in which promises are kept.

My face and I traversed all the cracks and crevices that underscored the fragility, fear, and everyday apprehension yet pointed above all towards happiness.

the traveler and the mapmaker

I feared travel and uncertain arrivals at cities with ports. I
feared hearing strangers. That is why I preferred to sit on the
edge of the road and listen to the stories, songs, and fables
of others. That is how I came to know unimagined rivers,
pyramids, and minarets, until one day I decided to create my
own world. I studied the secrets of cartography and palmistry,
drew maps and imagined compasses to help me reach longed-
for grottoes. I did not worry about losing my way as I traversed
labyrinths. I felt certain I would find what I sought and that
I would come to know the night, a desired caress along my
arched skin. The map indicated certain possibilities: it made
me see the beauty of cities and forests. The world fit in my
hands, the ones I myself had drawn. I finally felt lovely, and I
navigated freely with a crystal compass, a violet pen, and the
wind in my hair as protective guides. I lost my fear of uncertainty and knew that I would always find what I had imagined
at the root of my dreams, with God's light illuminating things
like a brilliant lamp.

cities of water

I loved the cities of water—Alexandria, Beirut, Recife, and
Viña del Mar—but I did not linger in their ports or bays.
Instead I imagined the sea, the water, or a path headed to the
shore across all distances.

Beyond a change in fortune, beyond returning home, it was the illusion of an arrival, the journey across fields and small hills, like delicate caresses thrilling my body. Then I would enter the cities like someone leaving the concave arc of sleep.

traveling

For me traveling was that sensation of awaking alone in a hotel, then facing the window in expectation of a new day. In the silence of the room, I imagined my movements: small steps, the moist tiles caressing my feet, and the recognition of noises from outside my own being. I approached a fountain in the middle of a plaza and felt precisely that, the other life, the lives of others, and now my own existence brushing up against my gaze. The pleasure of being in another place intensified; nothing reminded me of what I was or had been. Traveling is a present, a walk along the abyss of dreams. It replaces past memories with new adventures. The pleasure of a journey lies in knowing one is guided only by uncertainty and that no mirror will reflect yesterday's face. Instead every mirror points towards doubt and paths strewn with brambles, labyrinths, and pyramids of fire.

I knew that traveling was like making love, the confidence of a body always unknown, adding other landscapes to the soul, allowing life to be an impulse, a flow of dreams. Traveling meant not desiring the quotidian. It was an obsession with astonishment, the wished-for tracks that lead into forbidden enclosures, the discovery of a waterfall, a breath of light and freshness.

the treasures of arrival

And as I traveled I became smaller and smaller. More than progress I treasured arrivals so that I could begin to narrate my increasingly uncertain and distant journeys.

~ *southern shores*

chile

I wanted to dream about my country, draw near to her as if
for the first time, with the innocence of the little girl who
asks where they put the dead people. My country was a sharp
desert where women rested upon a silenced history and eight
hundred inactive volcanoes. I wanted to know that long and
narrow piece of land, to traverse her body like that of a young
woman yet to bear children. It was then that I came upon the
brutal beauty and horror of the poppy fields.

santiago

Day and night I think about my city. I dream the dream of
all exiles. I lose the keys needed to cross its thresholds. I
arrive darkly and no one recognizes me, or perhaps I am the
one who does not recognize the cities of memory, as they are
fragile and fleeting. I want to remember my city, the coastal
evenings when I would happily tumble outside to gaze all
night long at the stars and name each one out loud. I remember how we used to have to whisper in each other's ears the
names of dear friends, those who had left and now spent every
night in other houses. They dyed their hair and painted their
fingernails, but their souls remained unchanged.

You ask me about my city, and I must tell you. At night men
with gray faces, names, and boots patrolled the streets and
clumsily entered the houses of the poor, taking away defense-

less men: bread makers, firemen, trash collectors, anyone whose crime was goodness. I remember this because I could no longer go out at night to gaze at the stars. Paralyzed, my mother, grandmother, and I listened to the mute darkness and feared those nebulous stars that filled the sky, intent on pursuing and imprisoning us. How many nights did I lie suspended in bed, terrified that they might come for me? I could hear the dogs bark as the night grew deeper and more restless. I always asked myself if it was my turn.

That was the city of Santiago, the city in which I never felt like a guest. I loved Santiago madly, and I perfumed my entire body so that happiness might cling to my skin and heal it. That was my beloved city where I learned to read Hebrew and Spanish, where I recited the Lord's Prayer. And then someone knocked at our door and predicted our flight. We quickly left to become other people, to live restlessly in the shifting zones of memory.

the city of childhood

Between familiar and remote the landscape adjusts itself to the body. Hands impart warmth to the secrets of childhood. They were agile and diminutive. That's how I remember my simple and furrowed hands, groping the immensity of things, climbing up into the highest tops of the most gigantic trees. Now I feel that my hands are like bushes, small tangles of leaves upon the grass.

I return to my country with a mixture of longing and nostalgia, estrangement and ire. I recognize myself in the signs of my body; I perceive odors from the past and the present. There is a knot of wind at my temples. My relatives have aged. The giants of yesteryear are diminutive men speaking in very loud voices; they have grown small, deaf, and blind. They have remained suspended in the memory of what I was, a tiny girl who loved to dance. Now I tower over all of them. Is it possible to return to one's country or to the garden of childhood?

Impermanence is a self-fulfilling prophecy for the traveler who goes back, especially if she is a small traveler who was expelled from her garden. I return, but I do not recognize myself. In the dreams I invoke, I see myself standing in the shadows. I knock on doors and no one answers. I open windows only to let in the winter fog. At night I return to the room in which I see my dreams and poetry. I pause silently and imagine it illuminated. I understand that travelers can never go home. They must constantly move along. The only possible country is like a river: an outlet for the imagination.

home

Then I arrived at the house where I had lived as a child. It was waiting for me because I had looked for it. The front door opened like a loving hand. My feet recognized the pebbles and the playful grass. The lizards left their dwellings, and the stone threshold greeted me with a bow. Then I knew that

I was at once a child and an old woman, suspended between two bridges, two hemispheres, and two stories. I suddenly realized that one recovers what is lost along the way, that it is enough to remember who we once were, to see yesterday's objects reappear in the most sacred places within our memory or the heart's grottos of misfortune, like a sigh.

the fairy

Self-assured, with her small magic wand and cape of stars, she decided to head out in search of what she had seen and named. Along the way she found God, who asked her nothing. He let her walk among the dunes between the sea and the meadows. Suddenly she realized that she had arrived at her own face.

Then she did not know whether she felt nostalgic for that plaza, bench, or fountain. Perhaps what she felt was more a yearning for what had gone in vain, things forsaken, lost or never found. Perhaps she was simply no longer sure whether she was a girl or a woman.

pomaire: city of clay

The road buries itself in the valleys. It is thick and profound. It forks and splits. Upon arriving in Pomaire, I have a sense that I have entered this city many times, arriving at a place

where women bent over clay create by hand sacred and magical animals, slender pigs, and ecstatic witches about to take
flight. Pomaire is the land where women dwell and dream,
where they celebrate clay, earth, hands, and everyday objects.
No one knows precisely when this town decided to become
the province of clay. They say it might have been one of those
afternoons when the women, accustomed to the rhythms of
waiting, decided to go outside and look at the broad sky and
the deep landscape founded upon silence. Only then did they
decide to select the most extraordinary caresses for their
hands, the most ecstatic gazes for their eyes. During the war
they performed their jobs as one does the tasks of love, slowly,
as if each figure were a product of the womb and every hand
open to the possibility of caresses. In this way, the potters of
Pomaire sink their hands and history into clay. Alone, the
women and their faces are deeply furrowed.

Of all the figures, I love the one made by the potter who
sculpts generous shapes. She laughs, moans, and sighs; her
arms embrace children and the melodies of dark guitars.
The country potter smells like fruit, and her body is round
like happiness. When I think about my country, I dream of
Pomaire, where I went as a girl and fell in love with the hands
of the women. They were hands that caressed, fed, worked the
earth, and covered children at rest. Those hands were compassionate like the women themselves, and I was very happy
to travel to that town at the bottom of the hills, where solitude
could be heard like the wind. But in the distance I could also
make out the voices of the women bent over clay, over the

heart of the forest, over the night. Their outstretched hands were ready to receive the unpredictable, life, the rhythmical movement of clay over their dark and clear bodies, over the humid earth, like love.

isla negra

I always loved Isla Negra, which is neither an island nor black. It is but a fishing village some sixty kilometers from Santiago. To get there one must cross a tiny, narrow bridge like the body of a thin woman forgotten during a summer storm. Once across, the traveler is in Isla Negra. There were no paved streets, no electricity, only real and imagined moons. Each morning there was only silence, sun, and intense sea air in the streets, and at night the footsteps of those men and women in love headed towards the ravines where they would kiss. I always loved Isla Negra because there I learned about my body's ability to feel, to recognize and recover odors, to grow. At night we went to a small club where everyone—fishermen, wealthy children, us—gathered to dance, abandoning our bodies to the pitch of youthful love and passion. Later we would head home along the winding streets, each cobblestone bright as an agate, the fire in our bodies lighting the way.

I always return to Isla Negra in my imagination. Only there and only then did I feel the thickness of time beyond time, as if there were no point in rushing, as if history, dimension, and beauty had been restored to all things, alive and dead. Why do we love certain places and despise others? How do travelers choose the places of love, the trajectory of life, which arcs like a leaning tree? In what season do passion and memory dwell?

Isla Negra was full of walks and rituals that we alone mastered. We went to the Princess Rock where fishermen drowned themselves for love. Another day we visited the silent and small women who tell their stories through wool. They embroider landscapes, the harvest, the sowing, the May Cross—life amid the colored waters. We visited people we loved and the landscapes they created. My entire childhood I spent every summer in Isla Negra, where nights and days repeated themselves, where we sought the repetitive and constant exercise of creating memories. We were happy in Isla Negra. Once we crossed the bridge, we had arrived at summer's ceremonies. There I could remember who I was, a child. That is why one loves certain places where time not only stands still for us but for others as well, where the beating of the fireflies is also the beating of one's heart.

neruda in isla negra

We used to see *el poeta* walk along the sand and wrinkled stones. He watched the ocean for hours. Sometimes he gave us poems, lost leaves from absent, wandering plants. He was the poet of the beaches and the agates, don Pablo Neruda. He lived in Isla Negra. No one knew why that island that was not an island was called so. No one knew why it was termed black. Were poetry's caprices or virtues to blame? I began to learn not to put faith in maps and cartography. Best to get directions from the old women of the village, the ones who know the streets and could say go up that hill, turn left, touch your ear, sneeze twice, climb a staircase leading nowhere, and when you reach the top, ask for the black island that is neither an island nor black.

That's how I found out that real directions are in the sighs of the soothsayers. I learned that traveling women have only to follow the far-off song of women finding shelter in the shadows. That's how I got to Isla Negra, where Pablo Neruda was waiting for me. When I greeted him, he invited me to ring the bells of his island and in that way decipher the wind's alphabet and paint box. I arrived because I had to, unexpectedly, unsure of my destination, as if everyone were expecting me, as if I were the most longed for guest, warmly invited into those regions free of fog and full of clear days and poetry.

When I returned to my country and my language, a familiar wind furrowed my brow, and the ocean told me what I already knew. I recognized the blind men begging for bread and mercy on the same corners, and I wished, intensely, that I had never left home, that I had never ventured into other cities. I wanted to have stayed there amid all that I loved and knew, to have always woken up in the same city and greeted the same beggars. Our flight had left me homeless, my childish heart bleeding. I still have the heart of a child, and as if absent, it wants desperately to recognize itself and to know that there is an order

to the world. Lost, I followed the mist through cities of fog
where I could not recognize the flowers or the birds and I felt
like someone else. Once I came back, however, I knew that
I was from there, that place where I was neither a guest nor
a traveler, one of many thousands of women building a fire,
sweeping the avenues, or opening her home to strangers.

the city of foreigners

When she had to leave her country suddenly, she remembered
its infinite horizon and felt the dawn in her hands. She did
not know whether her eyes could contain the size of the sea or
her tears. No one was able to recognize her. She imagined she
was a leaf or a nut in the dark territory of a silent mouth.

She always felt strange as she stood outside and knocked
upon the many doors that were closed to her. She learned
to accept her destiny, that of a foreign woman, a wandering
Jew paying tribute to her origins. And wherever she lived she
summoned the voice and rhythm of happiness, but she lived
as a foreigner, always ready to flee.

osorno

My mother never wanted to be a heroine. Swinging between
tightly shorn trees she preferred to be the wind's messenger
in southern realms where birds could be mistaken for dense

shadows. She learned about the austerity of silence and the danger of words, changeable like her blue petticoats. Yet she was able to tell me, between murmur and memory, that the school down the street flew two flags: that of Germany and the banner with the swastika. They adorned her city, so distant and dark: Osorno, a small hamlet devoid of witnesses and history.

At times my mother cannot help remembering those flags. She neither questions nor answers but murmurs a memory of fugitive birds beyond the heavens, among the shadows.

the languages of memory

She always asked women travelers about their languages: rhythms, cadences, the intonations of their songs, their riddles. She asked how they remember beloved words, the language of women that will not belong to their daughters.

She never heard her own language. They stole her name and cut into her history. That is why she asks foreign women how they feel their language, and she recognizes herself in each of them, as if all such women belonged to her.

viña del mar and the pacific

Even blindfolded I would recognize that fragrance, shifting like the beating of the wind's wings above the hills. Since I was a girl I have imagined that sound, like the blinking of stars in the depths of the earth. What is the ocean but a giant heart beating in all things or a secret city of seaweed, anemones, hidden butterflies? Since I was a girl I have wanted to know what lies behind things. I began by looking into my mother's eyes, as if she held the ends of the oceans, the wings of ship-wrecked birds, or love letters buried deep in the sand.

At night the Pacific unties its bag full of passions like an arpeggio of memory. As if crazed, it rises over the rocks and listens to itself roar. By that ocean is where I realized I should remain close to the cities of water and witness the rhythms of blue upon the walls, the earth, all things. Sometimes in the cities of water, I mistook the sea for sky, the desert for water, and at night I could hear it reach and brush up against my window.

rain

The rain settles in Viña del Mar. The ocean, too, is a wet wall. Travelers move quickly, seeking shelter in hopes of slowing both their pace and their souls in so much darkness. I pause and dream that the rain is an incessant well in the sky. The poor who live in the hills, close to the sky, are shipwrecked by the rain as it destroys their shacks. The rain leaves them exposed to the most furious of storms. All they have left are the gifts of grace and resignation. In the cities of rain, the poor parade naked. All that lasts for them is faith, solitude, and implacable destiny.

reaching valparaíso

Midway through the day's journey along the privileged horizon, she felt the arrival of the light. It came unexpectedly, simply, like the wind brushing against her cheek.

She knew then that her trip should not be planned but rather open to the unexpected prophecies that might reach her tired feet. She understood the effort of traveling, the wisdom of arriving at unexpected places and resting in them all, not as a stranger nor a curious person but as a true traveler, one who recognizes and is recognized, who gives and receives with hands that are never closed.

The traveler recognized herself in my city when the wind brushed her cheeks, when the night offered her the sound of the sea along her body. Valparaíso awaited her. She approached the hills in order to name them one by one. They were not hills but rather stars descending upon the sea.

Along the way she met beggars and kings. They differed only in their dress. Without their clothes they were like her, adrift or in search of the harmony of the road. Some sobbed, others laughed. The arpeggio was the same.

city of wind and thresholds

One always returns to Valparaíso as to the innocence of first love. More than a city that overlooks the Pacific, Valparaíso is mischievous. Her hills hide young brides losing their minds as they prepare to come down from the steep slopes to negotiate alliances with love. I often saw women dressed in white running downhill as if falling out of the sky. I never knew whether they were brides or ghostly washerwomen from old cargo ships. In Valparaíso the wind distorts images. It is sonorous and it gossips. One has no difficulty imagining pirates and women in love or the house Pablo Neruda built here in the clouds.

Just as we all cherish innocence, we adore Valparaíso because the city accommodates our wandering feet and the possibilities of chance. Each day in Valparaíso is full of fire or shadow. Days and nights thread themselves according to the desolate and capricious wind. My grandfather don Marcos Agosín Smirnoff arrived here, the first tailor in this region of hills piled high atop one another. He came around 1800 with the help of noble mule drivers, accompanied by a strong woman from the Baltic coast and a small daughter who on these shores gave up being Hanna to become Josefina. She was to be forever from this city convulsed by nighttime sighs and enchanted winds that watch over the health of the dead and the living.

One loves Valparaíso as one loves Jerusalem or Prague. The city changes each night and day. It is difficult to tell time in Valparaíso. Her inhabitants often stop in their tracks, astounded by the sight of a burro carrying fresh milk and morning flowers or an intrepid and desperate sailor looking for love among the women of this port city. They wait for him around the clock with red carnations peeking from behind an ear or white lilies tucked between their open breasts.

One must walk Valparaíso at night. Night was falling—sunset like a red ribbon, lights blinking like stars upon the hills—when my great-grandmother Helena arrived in this city on a fourth-class ship from Hamburg. Family members who had escaped the fires and the pogroms came to fetch her. The women carried fresh bread and wore white shawls. I will stay here, Helena said of this foreign and crazy land, free of wars, its hills full of flowers and wild houses.

Each time I return to Chile, I go back to Valparaíso, her disturbing fragrance of magical hills, fish, and poverty. I take heart that people here seem untouched by vanity and consumerism. In Valparaíso the cobblers, bakers, prostitutes, sailors, and stevedores derive happiness from vocations rendered noble by their utility. Faces in Valparaíso are unmarked by the frenetic pace of postmodern life. They are peaceful, undisturbed, calm, as if the salt had preserved the fissures of their skin. The once-glorious waterfront now exudes the sadness of old age. Small boats loaded with young people in love sail out into the bay. An elderly man plays old and new songs. The waves, too, are a nexus of past and present as people continue to love their port city as much as they always have.

How could one not love Valparaíso? How could I forget that my great-grandfather Marcos founded an Israelite community aid center there, calling it the "Valparaíso Russian Community Center" because being Jewish meant being afraid? From his small shack on the dock, great-grandfather Marcos controlled the arrival and departure of new immigrants. He never forgot that he, too, had crossed the Andes on the back of a mule to get to Chile, and yet he followed his intuition and forbade entry to those strangers whose faces made him uneasy. One day a man covered in gold buttons, like a Prussian, appeared on the dock. Right away he made my great-grandfather angry and so was denied entry. What happened next is part of Agosín family lore. The rejected man sought entry on the other side of the continent, in Buenos Aires, and there he met and married my great-grandfather's cousin.

Every family has stories that are comforting and stories that are disturbing. My family will always be rooted in Valparaíso where, ten years before his mother, Helena, arrived, Joseph Halpern stood on a street named for the British and under the spell of fog, fires, and mischievous women, announced, as Helena would, "Here I will stay."

Joseph Halpern was said to be a strange German. He was too polite. According to my Russian aunts, he was a Viennese gentleman who loved to kiss the hands of sweet women. He especially loved the hand of my grandmother Josefina, whose father, Marcos, insisted she accept the crazy German, who in the end was neither crazy nor German but simply a good Jewish man.

I invite you to Valparaíso, a place of promises like all ports of entry. You will always be received by the four winds, and you will see strange women fluttering from houses and empty balconies. It will often be impossible to recognize their faces. You will not know whether they are ghosts or good women, but you will see them whenever the hollowed-out night signals lost ships. Things are neither light nor dark in Valparaíso, a city whipped by wind, a city where sounds become confused with the footsteps of ghosts that live in the pointed hills or in the bowels of certain illuminated boats that at nighttime sigh your name.

the lights of valparaíso

In the peace of the evening I settle my gaze on the lights of Valparaíso. They gesture like small lanterns offering the most generous of gifts. They possess a blue and startling beauty. I wonder about the inhabitants of those hills, their sad surroundings, their footsteps of mourning and light. I wonder about the young brides descending the hills barefoot and the bored men swaying from too much drink. The lights of Valparaíso tell stories. They are small petals in a nighttime tapestry. I love them above all others, and I see myself reflected in them as in a mirror devoured by the insistence of memory. The lights of Valparaíso envelop me like a desire. My grandparents came here, and tonight they are with me.

phantom ships

And with her eyes closed she knew that all returns
would lead to Valparaíso, to the coast along which her eyes
sank the phantom ships that spirited her grandmother away
from war. She knew that only there, amid the constellation of
countless stars and flames that surge on calm afternoons,
would she feel safe, never uncertain, with her memories, her
handkerchiefs of water, her girlhood and old age in perpetual
eclipse.

~ cities of war

tamara and silvia

Why did we go to Prague? Do we choose the cities of memory
or do they—painstakingly, delicately—show us the way? Perhaps I was a child on a sunny patio in Santiago de Chile when
I first heard of the two girls, my lost cousins. They were from
that city of bridges and rivers, of silent stories and bitter inva-
sions. They had come to Chile around 1950 with their father,
having escaped the Russian onslaught. I remember little of
their lives aside from their names: Tamara and Silvia Broder.
One had an immense cascade of copper-colored hair, and the
other was blonde and luminous. They were the daughters of
my grandfather's cousin, and they spoke incomprehensible
Czech.

I did not think of them for many years or imagine them on
their first day at our school when the curious and the cruel
encircled them in that innate gesture of prejudice: making fun of foreigners. Years later, in Georgia, I would be the
victim of those games and taunts. Only then did I remember
Prague and my cousins Silvia and Tamara.

My mother spoke to us of Prague as if she wanted both to
remember and to forget. The places Jews inhabit are like that:
places of revelation and expulsion. I wanted to go to Prague
simply to be there and to imagine Silvia and Tamara's small
stories.

What can we say about the first gestures we make upon arriving in a city, any city, but especially one of memory? Prague
was an elegant and resigned lady, composed, her eccentric

architecture ever brilliant; still and silent Prague meditated upon herself. We arrived at the beginning of spring when wildflowers bloomed in the shadows and the Charles River meandered, giving signs of an accelerated secret life. Prague has always been somber, powerful in her silence. She is a still city, one that awaits invading armies without walls. The great Chilean writer María Luisa Bombal loved Prague, too, and she shared secrets with me about President Masaryk, who was cruelly assassinated by his own friends and confidants. Prague is in those histories of friends and enemies, in the story of the kaiser's nephew gunned down by the Nazis. The city is divided not just by the Charles but between invaders and non-invaders, those who agreed to be victims and those who became collaborators. Springtime in Prague reminds us of other springs, when the arms of students sprouted red and violet flags, when everything was dressed in hope and celebration. At that time I was an adolescent in Santiago de Chile, and I read the headlines when Soviet tanks rolled into the city and the Czechs were imprisoned once more, sad inhabitants of a history in which nothing is their own.

the pinkas synagogue

I began to realize that Grandmother had once lived in Prague and that she loved the Czech spring as much as she loved the music of Moldavia and the rosemary and lilies in bloom along the river. "It is difficult to return to Prague," Carlos Fuentes has written. "It is impossible to forget her. It is true that she is probably haunted." I return to Prague, and behind her stained glass windows I find the girl that I was, the girl that I loved for her vulnerability and astonishment. Now I have returned to this city where a great silence breathes. I have brought my parents as they once brought me. The tangle of generations travels diverse streets. I bring them to this city unaware that they, too, have dreamed about it.

The cafés of Prague are as silent as the clock statues that appear and fade with the changing light. These small allegorical figures represent avarice and vanity. They are like the residents of Prague, who observe years, months, days, sunsets, and new moons. Prague is a city of alchemists, a universe of geometric centers. But Prague is also random, as when I walked along the Malastrana and suddenly came to the Stare Mesto, where every road was filled with the sound of majestic bells, beguiling and distant. These are the bells Kafka heard, and perhaps my Aunt Loricia heard them too as she strolled with Grandmother Helena along the banks of the Moldavia past the ancient Jewish cemetery. Perhaps they paused outside the old synagogue at Pinkas to pray.

I visited that synagogue with my parents. We know that Prague is a city of fairies and ghosts. We bump into acquaintances from Chile and meet others from places as remote as Africa. The Holocaust has become a profitable business for Christians, murmurs my father, and I concur.

The Pinkas Synagogue in the old Jewish quarter is full of people who, like us, want to get close and offer a small tribute to the dead. The walls of the synagogue contain the names of more than seventy-seven thousand Jews killed by the Nazis in Moravia and Bohemia. The synagogue's second floor houses a museum full of drawings made by the children of the Terezin concentration camp. We read all the names, aloud and in silence, names just like my own and those of my parents and grandparents. There are many Fridas, many Helenas, and I know I am here to repeat over and over again that they did not perish at Terezin, that they did not die at Auschwitz, because this synagogue, which is more than the house of God, remembers them. As I leave I place some small stones on the path. This gesture echoes my country's stories as well as my grandfather's fables and exile. Perhaps my loved ones, your loved ones, and I are here to meld those stories, to create the footsteps they never left, to invent paths. In this memory I recall the lives of others.

terezin

Who were the others? What became of this groom dressed in black, this bride in white? Why did they not return? Where is the mother who asked the police for permission to change her daughter's clothing before leaving to board the train? The one-way train departed a station like no other. In Europe death has always drawn near to small villages, suddenly converted into extermination camps where nothing blooms, silence is and is not, and the footsteps of the dead are erased by the wind. I am in Prague, but Prague is also Terezin, that camp to which the Germans took the privileged, those allowed to create, write, and think. Did Queen Teresa ever imagine that her summer home would become an extermination camp? I should not use the word extermination because the Germans were always too exact, too precise when it came to terminology. Terezin was a transition camp, a momentary pause for those who crossed the threshold of life and death, a camp that prepared them to die, but with a poem and a bar of soap under their arms.

It is springtime in Prague. My father hums the New World Symphony and we prepare to travel to Terezin. I have never visited a concentration camp nor have I wanted to be a Holocaust tourist. But I must go to Terezin and put stones on the nameless tombs of those I never knew, those who could never be. My mother says that twenty-two of our relatives died at Terezin, and the oldest were electrocuted in a mad attempt to escape. Cousin Alejandro was the only one to survive. I call them the flowering branches of Terezin, but my cousin will not speak of the place nor of what it means to him to be Jewish. He chose the land of oblivion and I the paths of memory. My entire life has been and continues to be composed of those fragile spirits of what never was allowed to be, small stories that comprise the interminable essence of things that name us. Now in Terezin I have returned to the image of Santiago de Chile and to my great-grandmother Helena bent over a wooden table. She is cutting pictures from the pages of old Czech and German magazines.

I am in Terezin with my mother, who suddenly is not my mother. She is a golden thread. Her voice is that of an agile, insinuating firefly, and she lights strange and unfamiliar paths in the dark. She speaks to me in German, and I do not know whether she addresses me or Helena Broder, the one whose sisters lived in Prague, the same Helena that came to visit Aunt Loricia and the twenty-two dead relatives in Terezin from time to time as we were doing on this day. As in the abyss of dreams, where words lose their presence, I wanted to be there, not out of curiosity nor to pay my respects but simply to be with them in the most sacred of human gestures. Kneeling there amid the yellow mounds that fit softly in my hands, I placed small stones, shrubs, the stuff of life on graves I did not recognize, in sight of not only my ancestors but all the dead who inspire those of us who fight fascism. That's how I arrived in Terezin, that camp for which the Germans found other names in order to make death seem normal. They called it a transition camp because within hours or seconds those brought there would go to the real camp, the death camp. There words could not be pronounced, eyes gazed as if they were not eyes, and light-filled complexions, once kissed by the sun, shriveled and became spectral.

My mother and I link arms. I lovingly support her. Our tears flow freely. I fix her hair, echoing the gestures of those mothers who are here and not here, buried in nameless piles beneath the stones of memories that strange visitors offer them.

I don't know how to describe that illuminated, dusky place.

The air one breathes at Terezin is fresh and moribund. Nature is not immune to history. I am very far from God despite dreams that I am everywhere immersed in the ordered, golden letters of the Lord, in those silent spaces of what is said and not said. The sun is radiant in Terezin, and we, the living, enter death's seat of honor defiantly and in silence. The slogan "Work will set you free" is found here, as in all the camps, as are the ovens and the rooms in which one can still hear the tearing noise, where children stopped being children and grew old in an instant. I am in Terezin, a clairvoyant oven, and I look towards the sky and surrender myself to the fragrance of tainted smoke because I, too, live in that smoke.

God gave the Jewish people an obligation to memory; otherwise no one would have survived Terezin or Auschwitz. We return to Prague moist with the ovens' vapors, fearful in the knowledge that the sun has forsaken Terezin. We return to find Prague noble, radiant, and dreamy. Only we have changed.

prague

What happens when the rhythm of certain cities changes us, alters the texture of our faces? Do we remove ourselves to a place beyond perplexing history? We are in Prague with my mother and her grandmother Helena Broder who left Vienna in 1939. That was the year of fissures and horror, the year of rusted ovens, the year of her salvation. Does fate exist? Is it a predestined restlessness or perhaps the path of God along our bodies?

My mother speaks in German. We are in a café, and she recognizes the many varieties of sweets and crepes. I am fascinated and frightened to see her this way, so sure of herself in another language. But suddenly her body seems clear, and her voice sounds like a stream or a river. She is transformed, rejuvenated. She arranges a meeting with her mad and fragile cousin Alejandro, the one who was in Terezin where his parents and grandparents died and where he first denied being Jewish. He does not want to be Jewish, and yet he roams the fields of Prague looking for his ancestors, repeating their names, weaving a precarious family tree.

What is my history? Is my name really Agosín? How and why did we go to Chile? My mother says that the first time she saw the ocean was when she went to meet Helena, the Viennese lady, at the dock. Today I write to my great-grandmother so as not to forget her and because my memory cannot rest. I need to reinvent her, know that she is near, touch her up close.

My great-grandmother's name was Helena. Every once in a while she liked to return to this luminous and dark city so full of sacred ghosts. She had read Kafka, or perhaps come across him in some remote alleyway, and they had said hello as strangers who love one another profoundly. She took the bridge over the Charles River. The statues acquire the insinuating color of devils and gods; the silence foreshadows the footsteps of the dead. I pause and do not know whether to flee or to let things happen to me, whether to open the shutters of memory and allow these statues—centuries old, of immemorial visions—to speak. The statues along the Charles River seem dense. Would it have been better not to come? Would it have been better not to see my mother speak German with her cousin who flees yet draws near to history?

We had a lot of trouble getting to Prague—it took us more than fifty years—and yet it is as difficult to leave. Our hearts remain in Prague, that open and fleeting city. Nostalgia clings to her cobbled streets and to the New World Symphony. Kafka smiles at me and makes me go with him to the old Jewish cemetery where tourists pile up to greet and bless the dead they do not know. My mother insists that we should enter and leave through the appropriate doors. One is the threshold of life and the other of death. The Jewish cemetery is beautiful and macabre, the tombs in heaps, one on top of another because the roots in the earth are overwhelmed by the number of Jews forced to live and die together, forced to wear stars. I am sure that young Aunt Loricia strolled with a star pressed tight against her school blazer. Suddenly she was not allowed to attend school, and with their songs and Hebrew alphabet, she and all other Jewish children disappeared from the streets of Prague. None of them came to rest in this old cemetery in the Jewish quarter nor were they fortunate enough to die among their own community. They went to Terezin, where from their cells they drew and launched enormous butterflies into the smoky and uncertain sky above.

At night the Prague cemetery weaves a spell as do the graveyards of the LeBeau in Provence and the Atacama Desert of my own country. What country am I from? My father says that I should not forget my Austro-Hungarian roots, but my destiny was to be born in North America where my accent and my short height would be scorned. Destiny also made our language Spanish, and I encounter it even in Prague, among those dead that play with fragile remembrance. I am here in the cemetery at Prague, an invisible and secret city, a city of memory, and my mother becomes ever smaller. She is like a star heralding nightfall. She leans over the tombs and rests her hand on the letters that keep the names of the dead alive. The weather is both cloudy and clear at the Prague cemetery today. I have returned not to trace my family tree, nor to complete obscure genealogies, but merely to be here and to leave through the door of the living.

vienna

My mother said that all cities smelled like her grandmother and that there were roses in each of them. When she and I found Grandmother's house in Vienna, we did not recognize the steps or padlocks. There were no doors or windows. Other owners had raided its belongings. Other walls had held its paintings. Suddenly someone rapped on a tall pane. The wind was like the tulle atop Grandmother's hats. A carriage passed along the narrow avenue, and a hand adorned with garnets waved to us. Grandmother had returned, or perhaps we had, guests of an unfailingly accurate memory.

budapest

We went in autumn, the season of soft, ambiguous light. In Budapest the sun spread over the hills like the wings of a bird, then fell, clear and fiery, into the Danube. We love this city like no other because it seems made of small, invisible, floating bridges suspended by the whims of time. Rarely free of the residue of bullets, the buildings of Budapest have tamed a perennial and drowsy sadness, and her walls have kept no secrets. They have revealed all so that no one can say that war and those who love war are somehow virtuous.

In the distance, beyond the shadows, we could hear the lost movement of red violins played by men like seagoing horses submerged in the legends of the Danube. At times one hears the steps of the Jews, who at the very end of the war threw off their long coats, left Budapest, and sank into sadness.

Sinking like them, I walk through the city. My eyes take in the growing darkness. The Danube's gaze is heavy: lovers' shelter, refuge for lost princesses, site of extermination camps. It is said that when the Danube suddenly becomes still, one can sense certain footsteps, certain voices, and movements under the water. Some say it is the fairy that inhabits the Castle of Buda, but I believe it might be one of my dead aunts welcoming me to the city on the Danube and its echoes.

croatia

We approach Croatia after the rain, after the war. Sovereign, she extends summer over the curvature of the water. Light blesses Croatia and reveals her submerged beauty, the candor of her inhabitants. The ship docks in Havar. Slowly, like people emerging from sleep or trying to decipher history, we walk.

Along the road our hands and arms become entangled in lavender, its texture and perfume. Vigilance becomes part of the forests of lavender that cover Havar. Lavender offered the possibility of life in the face of arid death.

The women and girls offer us small glass bottles filled with lavender extract. I feel they are offering me the earth and its pulse. I rub the oil into my body. I imagine the women on sunny days, wrapped in their yearning for light, picking lavender and singing. This is what they did before and after the war; never imprisoned, they were simply the lavender pickers of Havar, Croatia, where the light is a curve above the water and the gift of survival.

When I drench myself completely in lavender, I am, I write, I invent Havar after the war, after the rain, during the earth's scrumptious summer.

ana of croatia

I liked her measured and restless braids. They moved to the
rhythm of ancient hairdos, stories of ladies in party clothes,
perched uneasily, somewhat bewildered. I liked her braids and
their mix of black and white, as if she herself were an elderly
girl still amazed after so many days of war, holding on to faith,
shining light upon our Saturday. Her name is Ana, and she is
from Croatia. Everyone asks her how many Jews live in Croatia.
We Jews are desperate to know that we have survived, formed
alliances, held the memory of what has been. And that memory
is ever changing, clear and active, a river winding through
hillsides.

She responds and laughs. She does not understand the
questions of Americans, whose unfamiliarity with history trou-
bles her. With the slowness of ceremony, she begins by saying
that eighty-three percent of Yugoslavian Jews died in the
Holocaust. Only six thousand Jews now remain in Croatia. She
smiles and tells me that she wants to talk about her community
and her Hebrew school, how she taught the students to dance
the dances of uncertain times and that they never stopped
dancing and praying. On Saturdays they made altars out of
fresh herbs and six-point stars. As Ana tells this, I think how
all that is left of Yugoslavia, once called Montenegro, is a scab
and treacherous silence. What remains of cities after a war? Is
it possible to stand in those cities and look at the sky? Can one
endure the winters when the women of Sarajevo burned beloved poems and books in order to keep their children warm?

Today I have Ana at my side. Her braids embrace me and say, Let's dance together because dancing soothes the spirit and repairs what is torn. But I insist on asking her about the tiny villages, especially those now lost. Ana swings her water-logged braids that are full of rainstorms and wailing, and she says that she loves the Jews who have survived in Yugoslavia because they do not represent death, because they are not the lost dominions. Ana tells me to go to her city, to walk with her along the edge of her braids. She will show me the path of the Haggadah in Sarajevo. I love her even though we have only just met. In her gaze I have traversed bodies of desire, languages of passion. I have drawn close to her face, and I have found a center full of angels and peace. Perhaps each strand of her white hair is an angel that lost its way along the path of war and decided to rest upon her, conquering widowhood and the buried bodies of decapitated children.

I have met Ana for the first time today, and we have spoken ladino to one another, fertile proof of the continuity of a people. She told me that we are sisters of many peoples.

dubrovnik

Overflowing as if deep in a prodigious dream, I told you about Dubrovnik like someone speaking of love or the body of love. My voice becomes thin so that you can hear me close by. Each syllable is a step, a pathway through this city of still walls.

They gaze at the sea without haste, they fall, and are reborn. They crash and sharpen the rhythm of the hours.

I wished to show you the street of the Jews. Forty-three of them remain, and they pray for us all. In the humble doorway of a translucent synagogue, they extend an invitation to each passerby. At night when my feet and yours became confused with those, and only those, of lovers, I described fragrances to you: bougainvillea, hyacinth, jacaranda climbing the cupolas.

I wanted your eyes to pause on those crevices recording the fullness of history. And then the war darkened Dubrovnik. The city, an ill-fated house of cards, shed its walls like perverse cliffs of ire. At night I cried for the city I had made my own, as it belonged to us all. I asked what had become of the blue nuns in the neighboring convents or the women who sold lavender. We found nothing of their fate in the newspapers of insanity.

And one day the war ended, as all perfidy does, although perhaps Dubrovnik merely slept and dreamed a peaceful destiny, her arms shattered on the ground. I returned with you to Dubrovnik, and my feet as well as my arms joined yours. We walked through the city and picked up strangers, ignoring what we already knew: that the remnants of war remained, not in the streets or walls, nor in the synagogue of only forty-three Jews, but on the faces of the schoolgirls who knew the evil of skies full of bombs and vile gasses, and on the face of the motherless child selling lavender.

Like me, you took this city into your memory. Slowly,

ecstatically, we paused to view her beauty and cruelty as if she were an old child in repose. Her walls still faced the sea, and her bougainvillea testified to her survival. At night you and I speak of Dubrovnik. You tell me you know something of war, that despite new walls and buildings, war remains in the faces of the people. And I tell you to imagine the bougainvillea and poppies descending upon the fields. I tell you to dream about a night that breaks only to burst forth with light.

~ gestures of memory

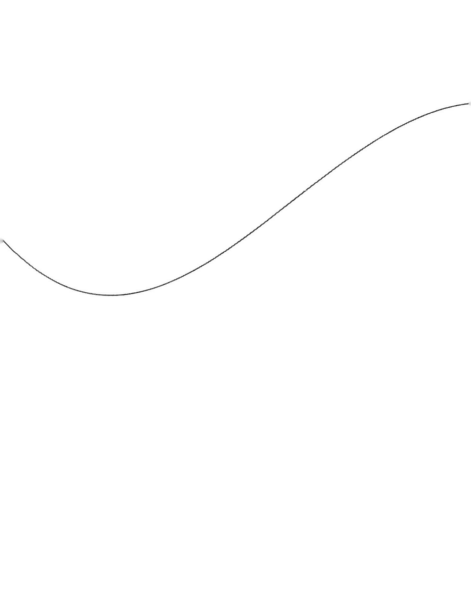

rhodes I

In love with the slowness of that fabled island of ineffable roses, their fragrance like an echo of melodies, I reached Rhodes. My route showed me cliffs, small waves on the surface of the sea that courts secrets. Someone sang to me as if from beyond the wind. There stood Julia, the ancient young woman, as small as a thimble, like a dream full of clouds. She had stayed behind to watch over the synagogue of Rhodes. She had said good-bye to the children who never experienced the certainty of death. She had kissed them and had told them that they should not argue with God. She alone had said good-bye to all the Jews of Rhodes. She had bestowed upon them a blessing like a living Kaddish and had filled their pockets with lemons and olives.

From the island's rocky heights, she had waved, like a frightened goddess, the slowest but most certain of farewells. Alone, feeling her way through puddles of misery and abandonment, she had headed to the synagogue of Rhodes, where wilted roses and the sacrifice of living far from her people and the things she loved awaited her. She had stayed there amid lost gardens, submerged in honeysuckle and orange groves, certain that this was her place, taking care of the dead and not thinking about the roll of the bad luck dice.

I had heard all this about her. I yearned to see her walk through the garden of roses and hollyhock and to dream about the olive trees on her star-filled apron. A gush of wind turned me towards her, and suddenly, like an apparition, the ancient

young woman of the synagogue of Rhodes stood before me.
She inscribed the sadness of her stories on the grotto-like
stones, assuring me that truth could be found only in the
traces of the wind and by fearless visitors who return to see
her as if reclaiming the most noble of loves.

rhodes II

It is possible to feel her
breath, a vestige of silk,
a fragrance emanating
from ancient and broken
times,
a fragrance governed by
orange blossoms and the divine light
of a precarious
return.

She, Julia,
awaits the visitors
each morning, afternoon,
and clear and oval-shaped evening
above the Aegean.

In Rhodes,
city of roses
and deer,
warm and full between
waves and thresholds,
we meet Julia,
she who returned
nameless
and without hatred,
unable to bury her parents
amid the roses,
without a lover to celebrate.
Julia is as astonishing as a ghost.

Julia,
guardian of memory,
caretaker of stories,
arranger of the dead,
she rests upon Time,
making promises to a God so often absent
and in her tattooed arms,
one can see and hear the sound
of the key
that opens every morning:
The synagogue of Rhodes
assuring the presence of the dead,
a fluidity of living visitors.

The street where the Jews lived
is darkened and oblique.
Another ghetto between the sea and the roses
and Julia tracing fragile paths,
peeling fresh oranges
and sobbing out loud
so that they will know about
the Jews of Rhodes
whose neighborhood
was once
a feast of small bells and olives.

I pause.
We pause.
The Jews recognize and greet one another
with the signs
of a somber heart.
There is an eternal sense of violence
along that cobbled street.
There is a perpetual shudder,
an inconsolable rhythm in the air.

Here lived children,
prominent families, and suddenly,
those streets populated by Jews,
that synagogue where they prayed,
became a lifeless tree
without meaning.

Julia shows us the way.
The noble and tired Torah,
the snapshots of happy Jews
of long ago,
praying, celebrating
the seasons in colorful dress,
and suddenly,
time seems like a void.
Faces disappear,
the photographs show
solitary men and women
bent over to participate in their deaths.

Julia knows all
but says nothing.
She is there with the eternal key
tied to her arm in the darkness,
and as evening falls
and the first stars appear,
Julia steps out of the shadows and
prays.
Once again she inhabits Rhodes.
She becomes a child
on her father's knee,
on a night
unlike any other,
on a night when life
was possible

and the Aegean Sea was a fragrance
of words, rocks,
and poppies amid the stones.

Julia knows all
but says nothing.
She returns to her house on
the island.
Tomorrow she should throw open the doors,
so that the dead and God's wind
might enter
the synagogue of Rhodes.

kefalonia

In Kefalonia the wind does not lament but rather sings above
the ivy and the light. It inquires after those things named and
unnamed in the sand, those invented and guarded by the sea.
In Kefalonia the ivy climbs the limestone. Amazed, we feel
life and its pleasures as we explore, awaken, and return the
image of a human face to ourselves. Pleasure resides in one's
privileged gaze upon the horizon of the perpetually open sea.

In Kefalonia my skin smells like jacaranda. The cracks
in each wall are filled with what history has left behind. The
cracks sprout poppies that survive year after year, offering
declarations of love. In Kefalonia I never run, and life sits

upon my skin as I approach the walk where I find a tree, a house, a temple of suns, and a delicate and urgently crimson poppy.

aegean

The Aegean Sea shifts before my eyes, the deepest and shiniest azure. The sky resembles an endless paradise among prophecies. And yet, in this deep and silent abyss, the voice of men calls to the voice of the gods. The landscape entwines itself with oracles, and the ocean is liquid and luminous, an unpredictable spell. I sail, and as I go, I recognize myself on this, my own imaginary voyage. Crossing the Aegean Sea means filling myself with legends, becoming other, feeling the sun on my naked body. I live in a unique, eternal, ancient, and always present moment.

My love for ancient as well as modern Greece goes on in a continuous, uninterrupted flow, like Persephone's dream. I love the women, dark and clear, ascending to and descending from the heart of each port. I love the cherry trees in bloom and the olive trees, their magnificent and worthy fruit reposing on tables, expecting happiness to walk in at any moment.

The Greek Islands stretch before my eyes like thick concave mirrors, fleeting windows on a very present beauty. There are no shadows along the way, only threads of light that lead travelers through the water's blue foliage. I love those islands and dedicate my days to dreaming about them, about their legendary earth and sacred stones. In those daydreams I prepare to follow the rhythm of the night. My shining gaze sustains me while I spend each day in contemplation, peace, and the certainty of the sparks given off by my eyes.

In dialogue with the water, amidst the residue of the wind over boats of an even deeper blue, I learn that to speak of the sea requires a previous language, a revelation of prayer-like words. Among those islands I allow poetry to become a blue dome over white time.

I make my way onto the balcony. I do not want time to pause nor to transpire. I feel sure that I will spend an entire lifetime submerged in the luminosity of this hour, this second, this instant, like an alleluia. My days on those disorderly and harmonious islands are unique, unlike any others. I give myself the gift of gratitude in the face of beauty, and I cling to the light as to the dream of first love.

istanbul I

Between Jerusalem and Rome stood Istanbul. My grand-father arrived here on foot from Odessa and was welcomed by minarets and a prayerful voice like a waterfall. He learned to recognize new fragrances, the subtle aromas of noble spices, the secret of their blends, the tenderness of food upon alabaster tables. Here my grandfather, a persecuted Jew, managed to stroll between the night and the jasmine. I, too, came to

Istanbul in order to recognize him, to offer a tribute to this
city that received him. I came to feel the presence of the clear
and dark waters of the Bosporus, to imagine him speaking
Turkish without anyone reproaching his foreign ways. I came
to Istanbul as if to a city of love, and I placed my ear against
her cupolas. I recognized prayers and songs, the fraternity of
faith.

istanbul II

Between the thickness of the wind and the clarity of dawn,
beyond the persistent sun at day's end, that amalgamated,
still hour when rest is a diaphanous light, Istanbul prays and
sings. Faith proclaims its sovereignty throughout this city
of water and minarets. The sacred is in every clear fountain,
where women and men, with gestures of peace, wash their
hands and feet, a bath of sheer gratitude before the prayer
hour. The thick purity is noticeable, luminous, and foreign to
the hierarchies of prayer.

The muezzin begins with a murmur, a primordial call. Then
the voice rises and becomes melodious. It coincides with the
rhythms of light. Istanbul, city of forgotten women sultans,
stands tall as if she were a cupola, nothing less, and those
who pray descend to the bottom of their being. Their bodies, alongside their voices, are rhythmic rivers that swirl and
become still, like fragments of faith.

I do not know whether I loved Istanbul. Before I had imagined it, and under thick darkness, I crossed the Bosporus with the swiftness and gratitude of a heart that loves and discovers. Perhaps I loved Istanbul because my grandfather arrived here on foot with his three sons and his pregnant wife. So many times I have researched the mystery of such crossings, the possibility of such an absurd trip. Each time the route has changed, and the silences become more sovereign.

jerusalem

As if happening in an imagined scene, I reach you, Jerusalem, and your domes like lost roses. Placid and restless, you make yourself comfortable before the pilgrims. Everyone who visits Jerusalem is a pilgrim. One prays for you and next to you, Jerusalem. At your side is a secret mirror, the sunflower of every gaze.

On the way to Jerusalem, one feels the ascent, like an ever-clear song, and the dense, yellow hills of Judea appear like presages of a history that debates itself. Before entering the city, I must pause to imagine all those who have passed over its thresholds, those who still die and live here. Yet beyond all sadness is an illuminated sovereign. She welcomes all visitors and sings God's prayers above the golden earth.

When my skin and gaze shifted to the dunes, I understood the desert's fervor and the angry passion of the sun. I dreamed of Cairo, Medina de Fez, and I imagined I was a

princess following my own footsteps. When I reached the sea
I understood all ports and their insistent fragrances. I lost
myself among other vagabond women destined like inverted
mirrors of water to reflect perfidious nostalgia. When I saw
the fields in bloom, the yellow flowers singing on the banks
of each brook, I understood that I might find paradise
here.

I loved the cities of the sun because the noonday heat governed the wastelands. I celebrated the light upon the rocks and
the wind in the pine trees that belonged to this present moment of summer.

I loved Jerusalem the way I loved the wind, the olive groves,
or the mirrors in my mouth.

And although they try, no one can forget you, Jerusalem,
beloved bride among the cupolas, sovereign star among the
arcs of faith. And although they try to harm you and sweep your
streets with ire, no one can assail the City of God.

israel

In Israel oak trees are planted in memory of the just. More
than shade they offer happiness in the midst of darkness and
layer upon layer of shadows. Certain men and women took
the only possible road, that of goodness. What path have you
chosen?

cairo

This is the city where days and nights melt into disembodied
voices, and footsteps become the once living tangle in which
happiness governed the wind and the sands. In the distance,
the wadis and the oases of dreams intermingle on a restless
horizon where men treasure their vulnerability. I walk with
my head down, stooped, touched by the footsteps of death.
I am headed towards the ancient City of the Dead in Cairo.
Muslim prayers are a constant caress, a breath of life upon my
walk. I do not find my ancestors or the friends of my friends.
Nevertheless I yearn to reach that city. I want to be where
doors remain unlocked, where the void and the wind mark the
fleeting movement of day and night.

But beyond the tombs like tall altars, the city of the living comes into view, and death steps aside to let me pass.
There among the dense smoke and the shrouds, the fear of
both solitude and communion, the poor have found their city
alongside the dead. No one bothers them. No one asks them
for anything, and death allows them to drink abundant sips of
water. That is how the ghosts in Cairo's City of the Dead serve
as noble messengers of life.

At last I arrive and realize I should give up, that time has
dug other graves. The heat of the desert wind and the eye
that besieges me are very powerful. As I lie down to rest my
body, beaten by all my searches, I decide to remain with the
living.

cairo's city of the dead

I am calm as I arrive at the City of the Dead. I recognize
myself as fragile, translucent, and innocent. I fill my hands
that seem to retreat in an initial burst of light. In the City of
the Dead I dream of angels and virgins. I am neither cold nor
frightened when beloved family members approach me with
fresh flowers and radiant paper streamers. I understand that
the City of the Dead possesses a splendid heart. It is a city
to be traversed slowly, as if steps were murmurs. I realize
that in that city there are no headstones or cemeteries, only
gardens and circles of dancing friends.

Then I go to where the wind lives among the shadows, in
the plenitude of the most dissonant void. I arrive furrowed
by dry branches. No one knows my name, yet because it is
similar to theirs, they shift gently in their graves. I whisper
in their ears, "It is I." An uncertain visitor, I have come with
olive oil, jasmine, and lavender for good luck and love.

The City of the Dead is odorless. Fragrances dissolve
along my perspiring skin, and the wind is a distant and sly
guardian. The city seems to grow cold with every step of
the visitors who arrive to look for their relatives among the
graves.

The city is like a shrunken bush. There are no bicycles or
children, only the dead and their subtle visitors on afternoons full of stones and rain.

I wander about the City of the Dead, feel the textures of

its rancid rooms. When guests arrive, who receives them? Do they come nude, already given over to the precarious art of memory? I never dream of the city, nor do I imagine it often. Yet on certain nights of dark premonitions, I detect that someone has visited me, the lights switching on in anticipation of an arrival. On certain nights I pause to rest alone and barefoot, and women dressed in mauve-colored tulle smile at me from the other side.

gestures of memory

The stories of the dead weave themselves together, beating against the sides of their tombs, demanding to know why they were dragged off, gagged, and blindfolded, their fingers sliced from their hands. The corpses crash against their tombs and sense that they are heard. Do you hear the dead banging in their graves? Have you seen them shine on moonless nights? Perhaps you have seen the golden trails they leave along the roots of your dreams? As the flowers begin to bloom this March I write and remember the dead and their prophetic light, slow and clear, settling beside me.

The dead beat against the sides of their tombs with their bodies full of stories and memories, bodies deprived of funerals.

Poetry is no more than this, a passion for telling. Poetry is a gesture of memory intended to cover absence, an extension of the truth. Poetry requires that they be named and found. Poetry demands to know the whereabouts of oblivion. I write in order to survive. I become their words and my own. There is little distance between the living and the dead, and I choose life.

~ touching the sky

traces

Traveling creates a desire to write, like a passionate urge to speak or the crazy impulse to lull a word to sleep. Traveling is like paradise, when I find unexpected words. Writing is like traveling in perpetual amazement. The unexpected, what is left to chance, is like a key that I find then misplace, a sunflower made of glass, and always like the pleasure of touching the sky with my feet and my hands.

mdina

Noble City, Silent City—that's what they call Mdina, but it has had other names, other rulers. They say that the Phoenicians came here with their ships and precious textiles. They fortified the thresholds and the portals so that Mdina could protect the island of Malta. Between the Mediterranean and North Africa, the island forges alliances, weaving and unweaving itself amid histories and civilizations that come and go. Noblemen, including the Knights of the Order of Saint John, came here to celebrate solitude. The catacombs conjure the presence of the living as they keep watch over the pathways of the dead.

In Mdina the wind tells stories as well, speaks many languages, and replicates the march of slaves and the songs of free men. Now they call it the Silent City because only tourists traverse its streets, asking about those who once lived there.

They ask about their jobs, burdens, and footprints, questions that in turn pose other questions. In Mdina I undertake a short journey through the dwelling place of angels and devils. Men at the center of faith advance upon this city like a hostile and silent cloak. During my stay in Mdina I wonder about God's fate amid the swords.

lace

In Burano, Taormina, or Valletta, the capital of the mysterious island of Malta, the lace makers work their ancient fingers to produce an art form passed from hand to hand and tongue to tongue over centuries of memory. Within this silent and isolated vocation each stitch enumerates the humble harmony of the women's majestic hands. I see them in profile, across time, young women and old. Their needles hide their faces from the cloth.

Liberated yet condemned, the women's memories are anchored to the lace, terse and soft and requiring the wise slowness of stitch upon stitch. From afar I see them facing the window. The world outside is dark as they lovingly perform the ceremony of the needle. Their gazes resemble rose pet-als, droplets of water adorning life. They lend an unhurried elegance to a time of tablecloths and napkins.

On the islands of the Mediterranean the lace makers are permanent angels dressed as women submerged in the secret legend of thimble, thread, and needle.

rome

As I looked at the fountain, it seemed to exist within me.
I imagined the water like the wish of a firefly in my body's
own beating heart. Again I felt the fountain and laughed and
smiled like everyone else. I wished for nothing, demanded
nothing. I was content to be there, looking at the fountain and
eating grapes washed clean by its waters. I was content to feel
the children, the lovers, and myself within the day, purged of
impulses, brimming with the present: the water, the grapes
brushing against my hands, my mouth full of pleasure and
delight.

the jewish ghetto of rome

Beyond the Tiber River and the clear breeze is Rome's Jewish
Ghetto. In the distance, indiscreet cats take possession of the
inviolate time of the stones. I entered as people do when they
contemplate themselves, perplexed, as if I were a timely visitor to my own history. Are all ghettos the same, or does horror
hide in the crevices of only some? Do they all retain that sense
of confinement and punishment, of yellow stars floating like
lost fireflies? But the Jews of Rome are not merely orna-
ments. Tourists avoid the risk of tracing the bold footsteps
and stories of this place. On the banks of the Tiber the women
of the ghetto live on incomprehensibly, their graves hidden.
They have not left this Roman ghetto, and nothing afflicts

them. They are too concerned about years and the washing of vegetables and meat, a favorite topic of conversation as they exchange recipes for the best ways to prepare artichokes. They promise one another eternal love, vowing to always live in that ghetto, the place they have never left, as they link arms and tears and sing in Hebrew. I felt ancient, and from that moment on, I did not fear curses. I looked at the blue sky of Rome and I became full of stars.

assisi

I took my parents to Assisi even though they feared arriving in a city so often the subject of dreams. What happens when people are afraid to enter such imagined places? Is it like the mad illusion of love, the sense that one belongs to the most infinite instant? I took them to Assisi because I had loved that city's saint since childhood. I had made him mine even though the servants confiscated my holy cards and felt my scalp at bedtime to check whether or not I had sprouted horns. I loved Saint Francis, his sandals and his conversations with the animals. But what was legend and what was truth? I believed in him the way one believes in a prayer.

To conjure Assisi, picture a storybook landscape and imagine the saint dancing and swaying in ochre-colored hills that match his vestments. Saint Francis does not preach, pray, or sing. He is like stardust sprinkled across the fields, leaving tracks in the wind and enveloping the animals. Here I felt his movements, and I murmured those light prayers that I loved, reciting them aloud at night. I walked through Assisi and the fountains spoke, telling the pilgrims that they had lost their way. One hears soft footsteps in Assisi and feels the weakness of those who love. Saint Francis's love contains the weakness and vulnerability known as faith, something mischievous and hidden, like sacred rose petals.

It is summer in Assisi. The tourists lay siege to the cathedrals, but one feels the stillness of the soft hills and the silence of prayer and faith. Looking in the direction of Saint Francis's road, I hear water murmuring among the thousands of fountains and footsteps. Those who can tell the difference between the various shades of green and the will-o'-the-wisps know which path leads to Saint Francis's grotto. We arrived there with the happiness of summer, and a voice welcomed us.

tuscany

The restful green of Tuscany weaves a memory of similar dreamlike shades, as when legends' summer streams run through verdant landscapes. I want to capture that green, like a changing and warm flame, a green in harmony with the hills, growing in intensity before descending to softly kiss the fields. I exclaim, "How green! I want more green." I contemplate my hands made beautiful by the gift of simple rings, like the crowns one finds along a path that leads from the most delicious happiness to the most clear desire.

volterra

I arrive in Volterra a bit fearful and reverential. That is how one must approach certain cities whose sordid and slow beauty is frightening. Between the walls of history and ire stands Volterra, the color of terra-cotta, perched on the side of invisible mountains. I have rehearsed my arrival in spirit. The walled city appears before me as it did to the Etruscans, a presence of swords and moss, indecipherable alphabets, and cadences reminiscent of the most sublime lament.

I arrived in Volterra drunk with astonishment and headed for the Roman Theater. I had arrived in Volterra as an uncertain passenger standing before hard and fragile alabaster. The Etruscans whispered their secrets to me in order to multiply the mirrors of the soul and its hidden acts of daring.

The sky over Volterra opened thick and blue, tame and wild, between the rocks. I did not tire as I waited for night to arrive, waited to go out and dream about the light fires of love on my skin and in my gaze. All night long I did nothing but watch the sky over Volterra. It was a blue song, a horse galloping above the doors to the city, doors that become endless mirrors, furtive entrances to monuments inhabited by gods and men playing amid night's blue dreams.

verona

She is not sure how she got to Verona. Her lip is split, moist, and she is restless like summer, like someone pressed up close or someone beyond all distances. She seems about to plunge a dagger bone-deep into the stony, boiling rocks. Summer in Verona is like a cloak on fire. Someone had told her to walk to Verona, to the Jewish quarter, because there she would find the philosopher's stone, the cells, the dragonflies, the secrets of all alchemy, the teaching stone, the wizard, and the faces of the dead, her two dead sisters.

The sun is a pebble on fire, a flame lost in the turbulent love of Verona. She arrives barefoot and hungry, dressed in brown petticoats, in mourning. As she climbs, night falls, and the street of the Jews appears in the very narrowness of speech and breath. After the night of knives Verona is alone.

Dogs cover the narrow street. They are a small pack of wild animals, lying in wait for her, expecting her. The street of the Jews is perpendicular, turbid, and so small that it seems to graft itself onto the perverse night. In Verona the street of the Jews is windowless; nothing blooms or grows among the rocks. There is no firelight, only the malevolent presence of time. Memory lies in wait. The sun is a hungry dog. The dogs, like men, surround her with evil intentions, delighted by her brown petticoats. The Jewess is frightened as she arrives in the center of Verona where nothing, no one exists any longer. The men force her to undress, they identify her as a Jew, and they make her wear a lacerated star upon her chest, deep in her heart. She did not know if she was dreaming, a warped textile of a dream. She did not know what was happening to her, or what had happened in Verona in the twelfth century, when the Jews of the Kabala sect were forced to wear yellow garments and stars of David along the paths and footsteps of their hearts. That was before, but today dogs and men still lie in wait.

She came to Verona to understand history, to rehearse the past and play the arpeggios lived by others. She came to Verona incandescently and beyond all time, where women do their chores like sporadic and lost fireflies, women made empty by painful times. Now she is in Verona, touching hearts, her own rutted heart recreating the pilgrimages of her sisters. Her body is drenched; the sun is cut off from its lineage. She asks about the happiness usurped from the women of Verona, the women locked in the cathedral, left to die of fright like those who died in the gas chambers and in exile. Here are all the women of Verona. She begins, in this way, to see them, beyond the smoke, as if they were the ghosts of anger. Their faces seem to have shrunk. In twelfth-century Verona, women lived in interior gardens, without firelight, doubled over in anguish, exiled by order of the Church, corralled by the voiceless forces of evil. In Verona she cries without always knowing why, and she draws near to the inner being, the slowness, the insomnia of those who scream and flee. Everything in Verona boils like a hell amid doubts.

She arrives in Verona and searches out the cathedral whose site once belonged to a synagogue. She arrives in Verona to

prevent the city from escaping the flight of time. She arrives
in Verona to find the tracks of her history lost in the springs
and to quench her desert thirst. She arrives in Verona alone,
very alone, like all fugitive and exiled women, like beloved
women lost in nights of violence. She arrives, and then she
leaves Verona, so beautiful under the terror. She leaves
wearing torn petticoats, her heart turned to ashes. After the
rainstorm Verona remains alone.

venice

I come to this city through intense dreams, bathed in un-
steady waters that pass over equally changeable bodies. Where
were we within the furrowed heart of the dreamy waters? How
do we reach invented cities?

I arrived in Venice the way one arrives at a beloved place,
without rules or obligations but via night's desire, daytime's
speculation, and noon's exhaustion. Venice—always with her
crackling masks, her palaces inhabited by dancing women,
naked save for their red shoes and velvet gloves. They are
looking at the water, sinking their eyes into the deep, perverse, and sedentary water, because Venice is made for love.
At night the illuminated palaces burn, and bodies open like
nets untangled.

I have also come here by accident, having followed the
watery gaps, the hum of the mountain passes, and the memory
driving me to touch the dream of origin. I want to go to the

ghetto, yes—the ghetto of Venice in the heart of this city of water, in the middle of history decked out in tiaras and silences. The Italian Jews lived there as early as the twelfth century. Capricious, they sang opera, yet dressed as Jews, golden stars on their arms. And yet, like all Jews, they were prisoners of history, yearning to be part of other peoples. In Venice they prospered as artful cutters of stone and mirrors that foreshadowed dreams. Now I am in that very ghetto of a frightening eternity that only seems to tell the stories of a God who dares to remember.

I am suspended in time, feeling where I am, intuiting the direction of footsteps, the way to the water. To what point in history have I come? I pass through the never-locked doors of a small synagogue full of tiny, almost invisible chairs that patiently await the return of the dead. Suddenly, from the roof of the synagogue someone emits a wail, or perhaps all I hear are the intertwined melodies of distant voices that merely approach memory. I meditate on those voices. They are small flames in the heart of the silent water, the madness at midnight and noon. In the Venice ghetto Jews sing because more Jews survived in Italy than anywhere else. The noble Italian police did not turn them in as readily, and they did not obey orders with German determination. The Italian police would say that the Jews had fled. The Italian Jews were cautious. At night they went from house to house, attempting secret directions, caressing their violins in silence.

I am here in Venice, and I have come to lose myself in

the rhythm of the masks. I have come to wander these narrow
streets near the water, streets that vibrate, blur, and merge
in the dense hollows of mirrors. But in this Venice of angels
and blonde devils, in this Venice of enchanted palaces, I feel
that the Jews are alive. They walk these ghetto streets because
the city watched over them, did not allow anyone to get close
enough to destroy their shops full of exquisite textiles and illuminated books.

I have come to Venice in order to feel the nostalgia of angels.

the ghetto of venice

I reach the Ghetto of Venice via the confusion of small streets
that crisscross the city. But there it is, marking signals and
predicting signs. The iron door that separated Jews from the
rest of the population is still there. I imagine children in tall
hats, their crowns adorned with golden stars, as if dressed for
a party. On Saturday afternoons the women would wear their
finest clothes, the harmony of their outfits reflected upon
the water. I see them strolling calmly along those streets, like
baskets full of light.

I continue along cobbled paths. One bridge takes me to
the next, only to return to the same circle, the oldest prison
in Europe. This is where Jews pray and hold firm to their
beliefs.

Now I dream other stories. It is 1944 in the plaza of the

ghetto, and I am facing a tree, perhaps a jacaranda. The violet branches resemble tears, drunken roots. I see them all with small sacks, possibly a candelabra, a kiddush cup of Venetian glass, all blue like the gas, like the dream that is no longer a prophecy. I see the women who earlier donned their finest clothes to gather with family and neighbors. No one—yet everyone—watches them now. Beyond the ghetto, life continues, a happy puddle. Children go to school, and none of this appears in the papers. But the Italian Jews of Venice disappear, the avatars of their stories. They leave the city in love with its images and palaces, the murmur of the gesturing water, and the sounds of the night.

Now in the ghetto I see only the names of Mauricio Renzo Allegra and Estefania Isolda. I stand in the plaza where they were arrested and place a star on my own body. I, too, want to fill the world, but with stars of light, not death. I pray for Mauricio and Estefania. In the distance, the Jews of Venice raise their voices in song. But I do not know whether the music I hear from the synagogue is that of the living or the dead. I do not know who is speaking, who is sighing, who forges history, or who foreshadows the truth.

In the Ghetto of Venice, the life of centuries, one after another, forges mysteries, and in these streets, each of which defines a life, the water laps against the channel walls, and the lanterns shine upon the firmament. The light is mysterious above this hive of the living and the dead.

nighttime in venice

Night falls over Venice. Who sings from the other side of the water? Who tries to divine pleasure? The city returns to its throne of silence. Placid, she reigns over the night, north and south. I hear only my own footsteps or what I imagine is the sound of feet walking through the Venetian night. On that May night I recovered my soul in a mirror known to me alone. That night I knew that I did not want fatuous praise or recognition. I wanted only to feel the night, to love it, and to brush my lips against it, like the blinking lights of a ship.

I understood that Venice was rescued and guarded by the angels of history and memory.

I walk, and the recurring dream in which I cannot find my keys or a lantern with which to light the way does not recur. I walk, and I love myself. I recognize my footsteps, yet suddenly I hear the sound of voices, an operetta dancing in the throat of an ancient young woman. She opens her window, wants me to hear her. Other pedestrians stop, too, and the voice is a prayer. A woman wearing red shoes looks at me. Another wears a tiara of glass full of texture and magic.

We recognize each other. I love Venice at night, when she offers us invisible gifts. The sound of water assures us that we are on firm ground. The woman in red shoes greets me, and the singer closes her window. I return home to gaze at myself in the mirror of my senses.

I have been given the gift of desire. I know the night and I know my body. I am in Venice, and everything speaks to me, surrounds me: night, doorway, window. We are what the water gives back: a cupola of passion, brief showers of memory. Venice is sovereign on rainy days.

spain

The language held the everyday wonder between fleeing and beginning. The language was like the sparkling jewels of illuminated manuscripts. In every city I, too, heard the songs as if from my innermost being, disturbances emanating from within and beyond the light. Then, in that solitude, during those nights on the cliffs of Toledo where they gagged us, I heard the song, the closeness of the syllables, the pauses between vowels, and a fire beyond memory and skin.

They were the songs of the people of Spain: in the fields, on the banks of hopeful streams, and in the blush of the poppies. I went there, too. I grew and became history among histories, made absolute and absolved amid the words of God.

deja

The fog utters its own language atop the hills. I arrive in Deja slowly, like a person who reaches the apex of a veil-draped sky. The fog over Deja lies in ambush and invites me to know Deja at nighttime. During the afternoon, lights blink in those houses of stone and legend. People return home, and their footsteps recall those of night watchmen who have eagerly awaited the dark. I always return to Deja like someone recovering what is loved. The nights and fires tremble tenuously, extending an invitation to pleasure. All pleasure can be found here in Deja, beside the rivers that rise and draw near to the sea, always distant because it can be imagined.

I come to Deja despite what can be imagined, but I must allow the fog and the transparent waterfalls to lead the way. Time does not devour; it does not pass—it only exists. Time in Deja can be touched and rocks back and forth. Then someone speaks about that winter full of owls on the island of Majorca. I also think of poetry, about those who have experience daylight and nighttime in Deja. I came to this island to visit the spot where Robert Graves was buried, but I remained on the skirt of that hill and recited poems. I thought that death does not exist, only oblivion.

valldemossa

The memory of travelers is bold and capricious, vulnerable and cruel. Few travelers have left as lasting an impression on Valldemossa as George Sand and Frédéric Chopin. Their arrival here in the winter of 1839 seems like only yesterday. Sand, a dazzling and brave woman wearing slacks and smoking a cigar, came with vulnerable and tender Chopin to the Cartujo Monastery, a refuge for priests, lovers of silence and herbs. They spent that malevolent winter in Majorca, where the mist pursued them like a dry garment, sleepless and alone. Travelers of words and sounds, they thought that they would find the peace of angels on this thick, green island. Yet all they did was sink into the fog that cut their throats, wrapped them tightly, and sent them sleepwalking through enormous and empty rooms. Not a single prayer could be heard in those rooms where silence was unable to guard peace and instead became the most subjugating of enemies.

Chopin rarely left those rooms that winter. He waited patiently, monastically, for his piano to arrive while imagining preludes and prairies. His sedentary, lonely tears marked the rhythm of his sadness.

Perhaps that is why dead angels, invisible monks, sharp footsteps, and Frédéric Chopin, his eyes lifted toward the mountains, are the only beings to greet travelers who reach Valldemossa. Legend has it that on certain nights a small piano can be heard, like an innocent wind in search of its lost heart.

in ávila with saint teresa

Your language was like slippery grains of sand, transforming itself, changing color and texture like a voice done and undone. The sand was like your hair, full of shooting stars and fables.

How I loved your company, Teresa of Ávila, during Castilian nights and dense Andean afternoons. You always came with me along the pathways of faith and of the soul, your body so robust, a woman in love. I preferred your voice to praying or singing. I loved your words, the wild mischief of God on earth.

Teresa of Ávila, this is not the real Paradise, and that is why you come and go so wisely, so in love, establishing convents and looking for the sacred in a thimble, a ring, your clear, barefoot, and playful order so like a choir of certain angels, subtle messengers of God.

On this dark and clear night when I have come to meet you, I realize that to love is to remember and that forgetfulness is the danger of idleness. Your lines are written on my forehead, your hands are in my hair so much like your own, full of ashes. I dream about you, and I love you. I am at your side, a walker and wanderer like all women.

I like to walk with you because we are both brave Jewish women building and inventing histories. Why did you build convents? Why did you work frenetically to found things and to do more and more? Was it perhaps your wish to be humbled, to work, to not let your hands be like two vain wings in the shadow of a foreign God? You made faith a song. The divine presence was in the olive tree and in the never-fatuous fires. Your hands were like soft flames, thin and calm as they rose toward the hand of a God that, through you, seemed less severe.

Teresa of Ávila, you walk through your city to the beat of the landscape, small ashes clinging to your hair, your face a wide mouthful of light. The asceticism of your name is a fountain of simple things like thimbles and breezes held in God's hands. We walk along the walls of Ávila, but for you neither time nor walls exist. There are no nations or borders. All that exists is the task called word, prayer, or faithful presence within your language.

I draw near not to exalt the past or the future but to tell you that I feel your presence in the light breeze created by God's eyelids. There you dwell, beyond life and death.

Since I was small I have loved you, read you openly as if you were my grandmother, aunt, relative: a Jewish woman who devoted herself to founding convents. To found is not to conquer but rather to set in motion a desire, the marrow of love, tilling the soil of the voice for other voices.

Teresa of Ávila, you have spoken to me as you move, as we all do, with the gait of an agile and tired woman. And yet your voice shows us how to sing and call out to willing hearts. You walk and walk. All of Ávila fits in the round cup of your rough hands. Today I come to see you. I choose to come on foot so that we will be side by side as we hear your poems in this arid, larger-than-life Castilian landscape. I find you here, my beloved and dear Saint Teresa of Ávila, and I listen. Your words are as light as prayers at a prudent banquet. Your language saves us.

spain in my heart

I have seen their names on the lists, victims of the genocide carried out by that general who presumed to be the grandfather of Chile. Yet at night he went down into the dungeons looking for Jews.

Spain, who lived under a Fascist too, becomes part of our country, our language. This fall, surrounded by luminous leaves and fresh chestnuts, we learn what became of Aviva and Robert, students at the Hebrew Institute, crusaders for justice and the dreams of a generation.

This fall I feel closer to Toledo and Verona, to the Spaniards who after each war have come out of their homes with garlands and red flowers for Rwanda and Bosnia. I love Spain because she has cultivated tolerance and because she has pursued, madly but with cause, the man who marched through our streets in search of Jews. Yes, I found the names of my friends on the lists of the dead, but I know the Spanish people are judging the general this fall. Warm and in love, they interrogate him.

~ *northern realms*

ireland

Why did we go to Ireland, my love? Did we wish to understand
poor, white Europe? Did we want to see the British chained
to the cult of their own success, their own passion for power
over savage islands? Perhaps I went to Ireland to reconstruct
the story of my own country, with its many broken dreams, its
clouded history. I probably chose Ireland because it made me
think of women out on a prairie, scattered by a diaspora, real
or imagined. Suddenly, as in the most sonorous and dense
dream, a voice told me to go to that island inhabited by fairies
and sprites, caught between war and peace, enlightenment
and discord. So we went, losing our minds along the only
steep road through nameless regions. We arrived in Ireland,
and the dream was fulfilled by stormy beauty, all green and
windy, with women leaning out reddish windows, as if to
discover love and myth.

Both of us went to Ireland in love with the dream itself.
You who had never had a country or language chose this wild
and noisy place, this island of rain and distances and water,
bearer of adventures and magical fairies. Perhaps you felt less
alone here, closer to the land and to the immensity of what
can and cannot be. I learned to love you on this island in the
wake of discord, insane misunderstanding, and unbridled
passion. You and I arrived in Ireland devoid of malice.

Since childhood I have told myself about Ireland, about
her sheep drowsing in peaceful, pleasant dreams, about the
soft and terse hills like the breasts of adolescents who bend

uncertainly under the weight of a new passion. But I was told, too, about Bernardo O'Higgins, the blonde, blue-eyed hero born to an Irish father and a Chilean mother. While his father served the Spanish crown, Bernardo headed a revolution against royal authority to become the father of Chilean independence and the head of our first national government. I went to Ireland either to verify the history of Chile or to make sure that my eyes were blue like his. What prompts us to explore foreign lands as well as what is most deeply familiar? What makes us move beyond watchfulness, sleep, or the perfidious memory of a story about liberators and warriors we desperately try to make our own?

We arrived in Ireland, and the country's dream of freedom took us to unexpected places. Poetry, embers of passion, and words bless this island. Suddenly I hear those prairie women, women from the forests lashed by the most irate desperation, bound by the savage nature of these islands of rage and poverty. Then someone sings among the seaside springs, and the wind rolls over my body and around my waist, etching stories on my face. The women are wracked by sinister hunger. I see their braided hair upon the green and stealthy sea, the sea that has always belonged to those who are sure they will find a way back to Ithaca. But what of the women who long for home? Where is their Ithaca? Where can they gather, and foregoing sleep, come to know themselves and one another? Is there an Ithaca for trembling women?

I mention the women in order to count myself among them. In the midst of the raging storm and diminutive moans, they were there, speaking Irish and Gaelic, clinging to their language. They were the guardians of words and wind, the dense heart of the forest. Their sacred and drowsy passion for words and language, a never-to-be-forgotten turn of phrase, allowed them to simply feel, touch, recreate, speak, and love.

london

I always wondered what became of Aron's sisters once he disappeared at the hands of Pinochet. What became of the women of the house, suddenly gone from our side? Today, in London, the general who supposedly loved the Hebrew people (he did not dare call us Jews) is on trial. He is the same general who, dressed all in white, recognized neither the dead nor the living. He is the same general who pursued Jews most passionately, tied them to stakes in the immense night, and tortured them as intensely as possible for committing the crime of being Hebrew.

the church of st. james

At the Church of St. James, the elderly women, diminished by the unpredictability of the weather, light candles of peace. The afternoon is tinged with ever-clear shadows of a violet hue. At the Church of St. James, I understand the melody of the prayers said in common and the power of naming God together. I watch the women and imagine how they looked more than fifty years ago, bold young girls singing songs of peace as bombs fell on London.

In the city where I live today, I take my children to light candles of peace. I whisper in their ears the secrets of the old ladies of St. James, those young, sonorous, and intrepid girls. I ask my son and daughter to light candles for the children of Iraq, the Congo, and East Timor, places where horror does not justify the naming of true horror. But I also ask them to light candles for the children of America, each day more un-done by our lack of faith in ourselves. And the peace candles, tiny flames, dance in the arrogant springtime wind. My children ask me about the wars waged in my other country, Chile. I tell them that on another September 11, back in 1973, a palace was bombed and a president recited words of hope as it burned, assuring us that beyond the immense avenues one day we would be free.

That was many years ago, I say. The candles remain at attention in their tender hands, and I want my children to know, to not be indifferent and arrogant in the face of history. And the old women of St. James tell me their secrets. They speak of the Blitz and the Spanish Civil War. Each story is sinisterly like the next.

I tell my children to love light. Then I promise them that after the vigil I will give them each a carnation like the one handed to me by the old woman at St. James whose name I did not know but who taught me prayers of peace.

oxford

I hear footsteps in the distance that grow longer or shorter according to the gravity of the night. I imagine those steps as signs of small and large crossings. All night long I dream about having arrived in a city where the dancing of water becomes confused with the footsteps outside time, an essence beyond any possible destination. They are the footsteps of those who seek neither arrivals nor departures but only a path or a landscape predicted in the cards.

I have never felt like a guest in any city. I follow only those impulses or illusions that allow me to know a city's most hidden shadows, the places of honor where love is practiced without premeditation. I also get to know a city by entering her cemeteries and listening to the sighs of the souls along the plains.

In that city called Oxford the entire community of souls showed up, from every kind of hell, light on their feet and astonished, deciphering the perfect space in which to slip along those twisted streets, beyond history. The souls fled toward the countryside, their mouths pink, mauve roses tucked behind their transparent ears. The wind, like an opportune guest or the grand owner of the empire—those regions invaded by moss and alphabets—boasted of how much her wise governors and passionate poets had achieved.

I devote my time to examining in minute detail the movement of the trees, their leafy tops, and that light from another time shaping and filling them. I love cities of light and souls because in the kingdom of the dead, the night is a perpetual heart, the foliage of history I want to preserve, the smiles of broken women and sweet Ophelias. I walk as if in love through the mirages of a city that becomes mine only in dreams.

bath

In Bath, Romans and Saxons played out watery dreams, imagining peace in the womb of a spring owned by goddesses and consecrated to the beauty of perpetual moments, a butterfly in the void. There in Bath resolute spring arrived early, and we found happiness in an English garden like those worldly Romans steeped in the wisest of pleasures, each kiss a tongue's storm-soaked dream. We rested our bodies among the hyacinths, lay back against the violet-striped canvas of creaky beach chairs, and imagined ancient rituals, the most sacred gestures of men and women intent on finding pleasure in the rhythm of the water and the boldness of life.

And in the English garden, subtle harmony of flowers, my hands and yours reposed unhurried and hesitant without the violence of desire. In that Roman city and that very garden, life in all its fullness settled among the honeysuckle. We were happy to reenact the story of all lovers who dream of water, mischievous springs, and peaceful gazes. We dreamed amid hyacinths and gladioli in perpetual bloom.

the mermaid of copenhagen

Beyond the mist, between vigilance and sleep, she is visible, from a distance or up close. It depends on the passion of the person who learns to look past the horizon that wraps every sea. She is dressed in grays and water, and her small tail sparkles. She invites us to seek pleasure and the stillness of deep waters. Her gaze seems almost human. In her eyes one sees the uncertainty of pain and the fear of dangerous passages but also the permanence of stone above watery undercurrents and submerged passions.

We all draw near as if wanting to possess her like a trophy. She does not reveal herself. She is but the permanence of winds upon the crystals of the sea, and like a heart she is tiny and capable of heroic feats.

The mermaid of Copenhagen belongs to Hans Christian Andersen or perhaps to all dreamers, those in the grip of a chimera. She watches over our arrivals and invites us to believe in illusions and presages. She is prudent and draws us close to earth's plenitude as if to the bottom of the blinking sea, violet and ephemeral like all of our journeys on land.

amsterdam and anne frank

I have come to look for you, Anne Frank, here in Amsterdam, not to redeem your sins or mine but to know how you lived, which meadows your mischievous feet crossed, through what cracks you looked at the sky as darkness fell.

They say this was your city, that you attended school here and began to understand the flame burning between your legs. But nobody wants to understand that this is also where you did *not* go to school, where so much was forbidden to you, including library privileges and illuminating books. I come to learn more about you, Anne, in the apparently normal city of Amsterdam, in this annexed country where you fought to talk about love's laughter, smell, touch, and mischief.

What are the cities of the dead like, Anne? How do I describe the cities of the disappeared and the innocent? I cannot possibly ask God, because children, too, went to the gas chambers. I come to Amsterdam to reclaim you. I know your address. I know where compassionate Miep found the notebooks you had filled by hand with your skeletal calligraphy. I have come to Amsterdam to feel your footprints, your steps across the canals, or perhaps to feel that the present is untouchable: my present and yours united at last by ties of memory. Why have I arrived at the foot of your house to find your name on the walls that reach skyward? Why have I come to the immutable edge of this canal to find your ghost demanding life?

We enjoyed our strolls through the streets of Amsterdam where no particular noise stood out. There was instead a great amalgam of sounds: my footsteps and those of my mother, who had traveled with me; the footsteps of the thirsty in search of roots; the savage heart of the night; the rhythm of the canals

sighing like wheels on a bicycle, slow and judicious, deep
in the Amsterdam night. Suddenly I felt a child pass by, or
a woman, about seventy years old like my mother. It was
Anne Frank, dressed in scorched black clothing and riding
a ghostly bicycle, dressed in mourning, dressed in marble,
trying in vain to cross walls and canals.

I told my mother what had happened to Anne Frank, that
she would today be about my mother's age and that her color-
ing was as dark as those evenings during which they fed the
wells contaminated by war.

there

On certain nights when the soul bends under its own weight,
I dream about a city of no returns, a city besieged by fear
and insane barbed wire. No one returned from that city, or
perhaps very few, dressed in the suits of ghosts and orphans.
Death delighted in awaiting her guests in that transitory city
submerged in smoke, among the ashes that all could smell.
Death stood in the doorway of the trains as the passengers arrived, some enraged and others mute with the tenuous word
of God on their blue lips. Barefoot, ancient children arrived
without dolls.

Death had clocks, compasses, and maps showing a single
destination. Death demanded booty: jewels, watches, and
gold teeth.

Sometimes I myself could not recall who lived in that city, whether a girl or an animal, a daughter or a lost mother. Sometimes I asked myself whether that city existed. Perhaps I had dreamed it during a terror-filled night. And yet no one could forget that city. Not even those who were never there. I close my eyes, and still I can invoke it, feel its chimneys, feel the howling, feel Death with her stolen gold teeth.

ainola

The paths undulate like possibilities that await us, our daily appointments with destiny. The crossing is thick with the brambles of dreams and sounds. Suddenly we are at Ainola where Jean Sibelius chose the hour of his life, the most accurate premonition, certain knowledge of death. When we arrive in Ainola, the wind is our first host. It slips softly through our hair like the most well-kept secret. The wind forges an alliance with the rain, its musical patter beating on one's skin, transcending the memory of what we were and the expectation of what we shall be.

In Ainola we must pause, feel the silence and the music that come from afar and surround us. This music is like the river that replicates the sobs of winter, like the tree that becomes full in the spring.

Here Jean Sibelius found his story amid the herons in flight whose shadows traversed his brow. In Ainola he composed his symphonies as one who elects a desired language of invention, of sound and cadence, of a word that is the ancient heart of speech.

saint petersburg

Prodigious and dark, Saint Petersburg nestles upon the crown of history. In the distance there are only imprints of foot-steps, pedestals among the ashes, cupolas of fire and blood. In this city Anna Akhmatova wanders day and night like an invisible guest, gathering words with which to love or curse the city, to tell what cannot be told. The night blazes in oblivion; the day is cobwebbed and shadowed. And yet Saint Petersburg remains immune like Jerusalem or Petra: she resists oblivion and learns to seduce her inhabitants. All foreigners love her from a distance and come to her through the cracks in her river or the fragrance of her lilies. Perhaps they come for her light that assures the continuation of life and reiterates the empire of her bridges, the majestic ingenuity of her beauty.

The imprints of footsteps are plentiful in Saint Petersburg. There the language of Pushkin and Rimsky-Korsakov, the poem without a hero, throbs in the imagination of a city like an oasis in the middle of a murmuring river.

anna akhmatova

Humble as if lost, I come in search of you, Anna Akhmatova, in your city of imaginary cupolas, along your river in love with its own silence. I ask for your paths, traces of your pilgrimages; let nothing escape me. I want to see through your eyes. I have come to find you, Anna, with your voice cupped in my hands, the sound of your story, the intoxicating strength of those verses that beyond all memory live. They arrive like a howl in the throats of free men.

Anna Akhmatova, I carry your poetry like a mirror. In it I see the faces of those you loved who have now emigrated into the void, into a fearless river, smoke and oblivion their accomplices. I seek refuge in a tree, the unpredictable aroma of lilies. I open your poems as if following your tracks, what the cracks in the indecipherable landscape leave behind.

And there you are, Anna, beautiful, intrepid, irresistibly brave. And when you recite a poem, the captive city opens up. And when you sing, the river becomes as mute as an acrobat parading through the purple sky. All the nameless heroes appear, the defeated Jews, the women with their rose-colored baskets of hunger, your son returning from the fields shining before your voice, your ageless hands of amber.

I have come to find you, Anna, here in Saint Petersburg. When I read your poetry the city is unlocked and blooms. Like a majestic and humble queen, your language is a beacon that interrogates and illuminates every homecoming. In Saint Petersburg I search for Anna Akhmatova, and she comes out to greet me like poetry.

the gypsy women

Ever more translucent and dark, the gypsy women of Saint Petersburg, invisible and stripped of their language, slip among the tourists and approach a city encrusted in the desert of its own history. Nobody seems to recognize them, and their gazes surprise no one. Unreachable and disconnected, they circulate through dormant churches. There are no church bells in Saint Petersburg, only the sounds of the exhausted gypsy women and their beads.

Neither luck nor faith interests them. Their eyes are glassy, alienated and perverse, and they draw near hoping for a piece of bread.

The gypsy women of Saint Petersburg slumber on the rivers above the palaces of floating mirrors. I approach them and ask about their daring and audacious travels. As I bid them farewell, I recognize that their lives are those of women in perpetual flight, always in darkness, always alone, as if in pain, as if translucent in the city of Akhmatova and Pushkin, now the city of sleeping heroes.

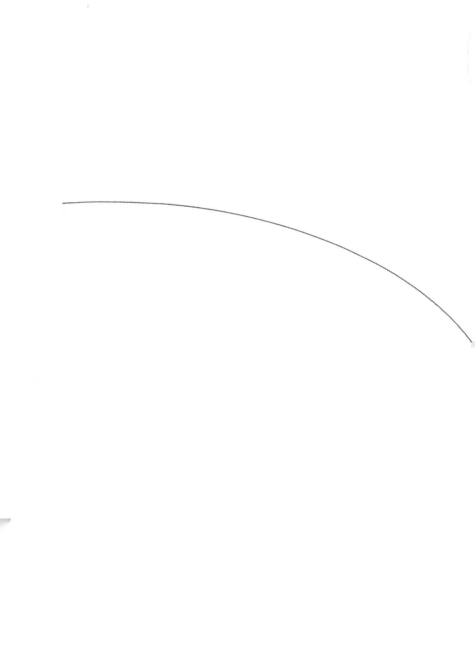

~ *america*

the weavers of charleston

Stooped like travelers impeded by long-ago chains, the weavers of Charleston tell a twilight story shaped by the shadows that watched their exit from darkness. In silence, to the beat of secret and hidden histories, they fold straw. They make baskets for bread, love, and fresh fruit. The tourists look on in amazement. For more than three hundred years the women have been rubbing, weaving, untying, and tying slavery into these baskets.

When they were slaves the basket makers returned to the stables, the dark wells, and the thinnest trees. They balanced indifference and moans in the shadows where they hid their names. Surrounded by fear and light, the baskets sang between their fingers, foretelling their freedom. Today I approach them, the basket makers of Charleston. My words become thin. There are no words for slavery. There is no word capable of returning their children to them, of restoring the many generations muffled by the plagues of oblivion. I like to watch them, proud and rebellious, always noble as they weave their baskets, extensions of their shining hands. These baskets are grateful for the bread that rests within them, the mute centuries, the dreams betrayed. I love these women, sitting in the Charleston market, whistling about life, telling stories about death, bent over the straw like someone who extends a tablecloth full of stories and dreams into the wind.

In the Charleston market the women and their daughters, and the daughters of their daughters, make baskets of love and presence that, like diadems, testify about history and its perfidious secrets.

miami

The city is guided by nostalgia. She intones melodies from a long-ago time. The past and a desire to return to it unfold like a flower that treasures the present only insofar as at is steeped in yesterday.

In Little Havana within greater Miami, men and women move with the slowness of those who remember. Their memories return to that other Havana that no longer exists except as a winter dream beyond a shuttered window.

Everything is a layer upon layer of nostalgia: the aroma of coffee and milk, the ripe plantains. And Cuba is a lady weary of remembrance. The men and women of Miami are like small, translucent phantoms in an even more transparent light. They drink coffee and milk at dawn as they take leave of today and head for the past, where perhaps nothing awaits them.

key west

I close my eyes and forget about the tourists that gather systematically at the most precise hour to contemplate the sunset and to look for Havana beyond the horizon. I manage to pull myself away from them in order to converse with Dos Passos and Hemingway. We raise our glasses to the only possible country: that of words.

dallas

The cities of America announce themselves suddenly, as if a powerful hand has sited them most inconveniently. They are stage sets in a made-up story, cities of invention and fable, unaccustomed to their own rhythms. The cities frighten me. They are distant, and I have to reach them by car.

The exile adjusts to imagining cities, possible lives that transpire within them. The exile rehearses the usual lack of trust, accustomed to journeys and losses. I arrive in Dallas with an enormous amount of curiosity about the city that witnessed President Kennedy's assassination and was later the setting of a popular television show seen throughout Latin America, a show that echoed what our own soap operas confirmed: the wealthy cry and suffer as much as the poor.

I wanted to see the downtown area and to imagine the road traveled by President Kennedy's convertible. I, too, come from a country where presidents have been killed: Balmaceda and Allende. Now I am here in Dallas, and I head downtown where nothing exists. The city is full of enormous mirrors that peer inward but not outward, the center of empty Dallas. The buildings that encircle the city seem isolated, unattached.

I am in Dallas for the Jewish Book Fair. Such celebrations in the United States are not like their counterparts in Latin America. They are organized and planned two years ahead of time. Nothing is allowed to interrupt the rhythm of our profoundly ordered dreams. And yet it is an order based on doubt, on speed, an order that can be interrupted by futility or by the careless ill will of others.

I have been invited to the book fair, an occasion devoid of happiness and community. It is a performance. Many curious people show up to hear the woman who will chat about exile and about her father. His story is that of many generations of men who confront prejudice, combat it on their own terms. But the women in the audience become bored and shift in their seats. This is not the American Dream. My words do not contain promises of patriotic love or praise for Dallas but rather the opposite. I sink into sadness as I talk about a country that never became ours, and members of the audience criticize me out loud. The women leave the room to rub their noses and peer at themselves in the mirror for the fifteenth time that day.

I am in Dallas, J. R.'s city where Kennedy died. I read slower, searching for a way to quench my thirst, to feel the touch of my voice. But there is nothing. Nothing exists in this city of mirrors that face outward while foreign men move through its empty center.

I have gone to Dallas to feel myself ever more disconnected and foreign. My smile becomes vertical and oblique. I return to the hotel that sits in the middle of a highway. I cannot find the keys to either my house or my room in this city.

angel fire, new mexico

As if it were an illusion, or a wrong turn by God, the sky was as joyfully beautiful as a memory, a son killed in Vietnam along with fourteen thousand others. A small plane condemned to the ground, ominous planes of war, the toys of evil men, accompany that landscape in which all was still and somber yet everything was in motion. The luminosity was as blissful as the liveliest expression of memory.

The United States has very few memorials, as if history passes unconnected to the reincarnations of man, as if the story of dead young men is alien, as if all wars are alien and have no effect on the consciousness of a people. But at this memorial, a father decided to speak of the dead young men, of the tragedy of wasting young lives by sending boys off to war so that they return as a swarm of inconclusive threads. The young men watch us from the monument at Angel Fire, New Mexico. I see their faces shift skyward toward the languid clouds that visit the textures of light. They are in photographs that cover the walls and, most of all, in the open flames that engulf the chapel.

For bold travelers I suggest a visit to Angel Fire, to meet others who have returned from a journey that usually offers

no return: the journey to the other side. A father of one of
the casualties has found an altar cloth full of stars for them, a
space that forgives those who sent them, a chapel that prays for
the future and does not harbor guilt or engender ingratitude.
All this was done by an Angel Fire father so that the memory
of death could become fire and stars. There I learned that
memory is the only amulet that can protect me from hatred.

tijuana

They slip through the night, a slender elongation of the day.
Busily they rock side to side, always lovely and clear in their
motions. In the rush of night and until dawn, when the world
is empty and becoming bright, the women cross the border
between Tijuana and San Diego. Lovely names, words that
have nothing to do with barbed wire. They sound instead like
a promise of miracles, growth, and possibilities. Suddenly
the borders are not imaginary. Despotic guards shake the
women down, remove their clothes, pull their hair, behead
their iguanas, and pierce their hearts. The oldest of them does
not understand this business of crossing borders. She knows
they will always be from there, from florid Mexico, dressed in
white calla lilies and songs like prayers or moans. The cities
and points at which they cross seem to belong outside of time,
absurd demarcations that limit the access of human beings to
their only true home, the Earth.

In Tijuana the women wear shawls of mournful gray when

they cross. In that other America, they neither rock nor sing but bow ever so slightly and reverently as they walk past the men on each corner, the police of human geography.

juárez

The night was like a precipice, with a hollow sound beyond all other sounds and silences. It was nighttime in Juárez, and the dead women of the city protected those still alive. The night did not resemble a typical night along the border. It resembled, more than anything, the mute lethargy of hell and flames turned into knives.

The night in Juárez was like a clouded mirror where Death rested on its heels and trophies. It had neither a beginning nor an end. It contained every fear and Death in all its amplitude.

santiago de atitlán

Like those voices that appear sunken in the roots of dreams, someone told me to go to the City of Widows. There I would take communion with the women and experience a void beyond any possible silence. Obeying that dream that seemed to permeate my skin and cling to painful wounds, I crossed rivers, oceans, and turbulent seasons to reach Santiago de Atitlán, where no one was expecting me.

I know how to find the shadows where the widows seek consolation and the most restless souls find an illusion of rest. They spoke, swaying to the rhythm of their prayers, the rhythm of their memories of those hungry men who died for their beliefs, their faith, for fighting. That's how this story came to be, as if it were a texture or a breeze. I arrived and sat down with the widows dressed in the colors of love and grief. Then, at that very hour, I learned to feel the space of wounds, that which allows itself to become wounded and that which does not. I learned that ceremonies need remembrance and memory if they are to make sense. This time I bent at the waist and prepared to receive offerings, tattoos, and gifts from a world beyond.

costa rica

The night was a transparent awakening in the company of able and dancing fireflies in a slow, thick sky. Nighttime moves to a rhythm somewhere between exhaustion and cautious slow-ness because the jaguars and hummingbirds have gone home to rest. The only gazes left belong to those who night after night repeat the same lone gesture. To watch the night is to see the leaves of the banana tree shine and to feel the rain cover the forest like a shawl.

Nighttime is a secret bedroom crushed by heat and tenuous breezes, by naked and shifting bodies, slowly set ablaze by love or the sadness of love.

The entire night rains down on Costa Rica. It is a night of peace without shadows or dead voices. The women do not search for their departed. They are like warm statues or jade stones, resting as they watch time pass. They measure time only by heat or its absence, or by lives made possible by the rain.

This unique night moves me as I watch from this restful balcony. The noises resemble footsteps across wet grass. This tropical night carries within it an act of faith, and the body and the senses throb as if sheltered by the most sacred of sanctuaries. The view is a privilege that brings us close to our origins. I listen to nighttime sink over Costa Rica. Among the thick trees the fireflies celebrate prone bodies, poems about words, shadows in the clearings.

santo domingo

My skin retains the fragrance of spices and the folds of antique silk. I walk through the city of Santo Domingo, in love with the enigma of Columbus's arrival from the most angry and distant of lands.

Nighttime in Santo Domingo is like a fable of shifting stories, like footprints in the sand. I remember the storms and curtains designed to ward off evil spirits. The night envelops everything like a sable, a sword, or the laughter of a shipwrecked sailor. I quicken my pace, but the Caribbean Sea is all slowness as it summons me for my stories. My hands collect jewels from the sand and replicate a complete and splendid beauty.

sosua

Late one afternoon I arrived in Sosua. The Caribbean was a
warm storm, a source of crystalline coasts. The breeze was
called perfume, and my body adjusted itself to the light of the
intense and fulminating tropics. No one detained me. Before
so much gratuitous beauty I extended my hands and arms to
receive the first rays of sunshine. Suddenly I imagined boats
and a Europe bewitched by evil foreshadowings.

In the night the Jews boarded ships of life or death. That
afternoon when I disembarked in Sosua, I imagined leaving
behind a vessel full of people eager to live.

They say that being here in Sosua evokes the flight from
Egypt. I am commemorating that crossing as I settle into
Sosua. The ocean seems immobile and present in every crack.
It insinuates Columbus's arrival. He, too, undertook expedi-
tions such as this in search of refuge and the possibility of a
new life.

The wind gently rocks my steps. Calypso blue surrounds
me. My eyes grow accustomed to the color, a blue unlike any
other. My gaze is like a party, a spell. So much beauty is dis-
orienting, upsetting. I walk barefoot along Dr. Levy's street,
also known as the Street of the Jews. It is here, between the
luminous wood and the windows that look like the sea, always
facing the sea, that the Jews built a synagogue. Here they
recovered the light and the possibility of life. The Hebrew
alphabet became breeze and song. The Caribbean opened like
the most welcoming of all shelters. The Jews of Sosua took

off their dark suits of death. The sun covered them in good wishes, and here, like so many others, they found peace and celebrated the ceremonies of light.

copacabana

Dressed in white, the color of peace and love, the dancers face the sea, not as in a ritual, but as in an act of love. Along the beaches of Ipanema and Copacabana the dancers, truly spellbound, toss flowers into the ocean, into the immense void. The possibility of faith and prayer is a song in the forest of waves.

bahía

In Bahía it is impossible not to believe in angels of good fortune. Children dressed as magicians approach and offer us red, purple, and yellow ribbons tied in vivid bows. I bury our hands in them because luck comes to those who believe in her, wish for her, and say her name. In Bahía everything is possible. In this light and dark city, hidden slaves arrived, sentenced by the color of their luminous skin, only to transform their fate. To believe in colored ribbons is to believe in the invisible. In this city, a jubilant and gloomy Babel, millions came to test their luck, to feel the delirium of freedom like a woman waiting for them, open and sensible, at every port of entry. They settled into a new life among many languages but were still able to rescue what had been forgotten, what they had brought from other cities to this one where everyone dreams it is possible to be happy. Today I travel, naked and drunk, all around the city of Bahía, where rocks sigh and tell stories. On each corner I find colored ribbons that predict a one-way journey, like a dream amid the shadows of chance or the cities of love.

teate

The entire country was like a prediction, a brilliant celebration of joy. Leopoldina, with her almost blue skin, drew near to tell me her stories. She had neither a pencil nor an alphabet. She only had the voices brought from rainy forests or the words of her ancestors who paraded alongside her day and night, in the stone house, in the house of memory.

She took my hands. She rested her incandescent gaze upon mine and sang the songs of the slaves who came to Brazil. I knew how to hear her, and only then did she tell me about that river near Teate, the river that for so many years celebrated the reunion of slaves who had been set free. Back to the river they went, to join the others so that the wheels of damned fortune might keep turning, to proclaim prophecies, to continue singing and loving at the mouth of the river, upon the caress of the river.

Then she took me to the river, and I heard voices rising from it and the footsteps of those who, once enslaved, were now free men able to tell their stories. She told me that there was no better talisman than love and a night filled with song.

In Teate Leopoldina made me understand the ceremonies of the water. It was within that infinite circle of human life that I understood the gift of freedom and those who live to tell about it. In the river of Bonfi, women and men sing and roll the dice of their destiny. The river shelters and celebrates them, and its waters become thick with rose petals.

río de la plata

He and I wanted to cross the Plata River in the deep, thick night, beyond the temperate summer storms. We wanted to make that short journey. All around us couples murmured, inventing secret sounds, but always with the same gesture of love between tender and perverse.

What happens to bodies when they make love while crossing a river? Does a body become as light as water? Does life weigh less when two people kiss?

We went out onto the deck. We passengers imagine unrealistic journeys and fantasies. This is what traveling offers: not what one does or says but the possibilities one imagines. Bodies in search of pleasure, fleeting conversations. In South America people generally avoid talking about dangerous topics such as dictatorships, the Church, and homosexuality. The recent decades of military horrors have brought a perverse silence, a disturbing hush. We have opted to make peace with oblivion while other desperate souls live only to remember. We are afraid of the nighttime shadows, the paths and foot-steps of the disappeared as they draw near after dark to touch the fragments of our dreams.

All night long the boat travels the Plata River, this beloved region invented by Cortázar and dreamed by Borges, complete with aleph and Kabala, the ritual of destiny and chance.

Was it chance that dictated the schedule of death in the Plata? Only now in the secret bedchamber, in the murmurs heard behind closed doors, do we hear that the bodies of the disappeared were thrown from helicopters into this river. Here they lie underwater, disfigured by fear and innocence in the face of horror.

We cross the Plata River. The night is a shell of splendid and victorious silver. The dense and malignant night sighs and sings to us the story of those bodies still in search of their souls. The entire river is a cemetery of shipwrecked bod-ies, of lost gazes. On this summer night when the passengers have returned to make love on the sly, to engage in sex as a privilege of the living, he and I have decided to listen to the footsteps of the dead.

Suddenly, in a dream, he takes my hand. We enter the prisons and the forests where the merchants of death lie in ambush. This Plata River is red, turbulent, and full of astonished fish that do not dare devour the good, blindfolded men, so small and fragile, who have fallen from the immense night sky. We are here to immortalize them, to commune and cry with them, and to listen to their song on fleeting waves.

In the morning we can see and almost touch Montevideo. The pyres of oblivion await and receive us. A sweet and beautiful woman named Laura shows us five letters from her beloved, imprisoned in that city. She tells us that Montevideo is still beautiful and that all the balconies in the city face the sea.

montevideo

Stepping softly and lightly, my family headed to the harbor, reconstructing paths, inventing possible retreats. In those days I feared traveling, for I loved the permanence of stones and the words of my language. Gradually I got used to saying good-bye to friends, to childhood, to the people I love, for no reason, without asking any questions and without assuming any guarantees. They were leaving, and I would stay behind to take care of my orchid and the gardens of others, lying in wait, expecting the winds of return.

I heard little of them and eventually found myself alone in a country of old and lonely people who feared the vicissitudes of travel, the uncertainties of arrivals. Suddenly I decided to board a ship, and at midnight I set sail for the horizon. I did not want to be a traveler, but my life depended on it. I said good-bye to the night, the moon, the caress of the sun on my skin. I would never return, or if I did, not as the same person. Perhaps an angel of history or chance would return with me.

In the distance I see the harbor lights of Montevideo. Not all my friends have left. I wasn't even able to see them one last time. I am on my way. My woolen doll and a broken mirror will travel with me.

georgia

During summer's sharp intervals, as if in a drawn-out dream, I return to Georgia. I forget to measure the rhythm of the years, the wisdom of the seasons, when my mother assured me, like Saint Teresa of Ávila, that better times would come. I return to Georgia, my first port of entry into America. In that first land, first landscape, I discovered the fragility of my childhood, that of an old child.

I return, and yet I do not. It is useless to look for the person I was and was not. Memory undoes itself amid the dark foliage that surrounds us; the cricket song is out of sync. Or perhaps it is my own voice I hear but do not recognize.

In vain I search the red earth and the stones like small souls along the road. Vaporous memory weighs on me like this summer that wants to end. I try to see through the bars of insomnia, and I find myself facing empty roads leading to mansions owned by southern grandees. No one inhabits the mansions but the ghosts of history and memory in pursuit of the deceased.

In Georgia the English alphabet settled in my mouth and on my hands with a southern accent. In Georgia I settled into nostalgia and its pain. In Georgia the humidity was a green alligator's constant language.

I return to Georgia. There they recognize me as a prodigal daughter come home or as an intrepid foreigner. I see only what remains of my mother inhabiting the shadows. As if they were small stories, my mother and I defy the shadows. There is only my mother among the magnolias, her green hand in my green hair, murmuring words that only the wind retains.

the tree

One never knows why people return, why they need to do so, why chance meetings take place. One returns as if going back to the beginning of a love affair, to perpetual astonishment, to the certainty of shadows and gusts of what we were and continue to be. Perhaps I returned, John, to see the tree. Yes, the tree they had given to you as a gift on that waterless island, on those Indiana plains where corn merges with the naked bodies of old people, lonely people. They had given you a tree, John, in a gesture of gratitude. You responded with grateful silence. No one had ever given you a tree or even a toy. You always dreamed about branches and drew them as if tangled limbs of fragrant myrtle were sprouting from your hands. Now that you were almost a man your teachers had given you a tree.

It was small. It seemed frail and most of all alone at the entrance to the old grotto-like stone cottage. You thought it would not provide shade and that it would atrophy during the unforgiving winter. You were afraid for that tree, like one fears for one's children. Your profile shifted nervously during that ceremony of fleeting wise men and you, like a Jew performing the ritual of respect, covered your fragile torso with earth as if life and death had at last forged an unexpected alliance.

The tree stayed behind. John, sometimes at night, while we carved our bodies as if we were frail branches, fine and fearful wood, you would ask me about your tree, whether it had grown, whether anyone watered or blessed it, whether other young men like you paused before its branches like rays of light. I merely listened as I clung to your back as if it were the trunk of a wise tree, as its blue veins, like sighing sap, opened themselves to the silence of your childhood. With the arrival of each autumn we would invent new ways to express our love, perpetual or ephemeral ceremonies. I undid your mouth as if it were blooming in the darkest immensity of the forest, your teeth like new branches and your heart a flower. The night was dark and tame, and you would ask me how I thought the tree was doing. Would it become an orphan this fall? Who would gaze upon its crown of fire? You kissed me as if you were wind, fire, moss. My body drew close to yours like a leaf, secretly creaking like travelers making love on a bed of golden leaves, gentle as thorns, a bed located beyond the impenetrable rhythm of the seasons. It existed only in autumn to meditate among the dying leaves.

I returned, John. I went in search of your tree. The city without a sea was there, languid and hidden where time had stood still. I went to the old stone cottage and found many small and fragile trees around its foundation, just as when they first planted yours. I looked them over, wanting to recognize them, as if they were old relatives entwined in sepia-colored photographs. I traversed the plains. Autumn was a shawl of love, its edges curled and tipped in red. Suddenly I found you, John. There stood your tree. It had not bent. It was there, straight and majestic, splendid in size but humble with gratitude. Its noble trunk was the color of your mahogany skin.

Then I looked up, and its spongy top appeared open, round, like the summer nights when we slept naked and you told me that angels would come to cover us. I prayed for your tree then, for the trees of all the uninhabited forests. John, your tree sparkled, smiled, nourished by peace and love, by the alchemy of the earth. It did not bend. It was tall, but above all, its top was like the breast of the macaw, blooming forth, hiding nothing. Perhaps an angel had spent all these years watching over your tree. It was a fearless rose in the harsh face of time and seasons. Neither downpours nor harsh winds affected the branches of your tree. Not a single bad omen penetrated its bark. Your tree, John, grows forward as if it had always been an optimistic tree, as if life were but a road to travel, as if its highest branches indicated the chosen paths. Your tree existed in harmony with the landscape just like the nearby imaginary islands. Its top and its trunk seemed to have braided themselves into a single ring, a perfect fit. They had grown together without deviating or straying. John, your tree offers shade to the children who lean against its trunk and seek its shelter. Above all, it extends the possibility of choosing a quiet path.

I have returned to see your tree, our tree. It has grown as we have, tall, resilient, and fragrant. From within me you drink desire and peace. You are like the trunk, and I sculpt and carve you with my mouth. At times you are the treetop, and I dance on your uppermost branches. At times I am the trunk, and my roots grasp the earth.

I have returned, John, to see our tree. Do not be afraid—it will bloom in every season and always bear fruit. It will give shade and light. It will color the autumn, and the children who play around it will press their cheeks against it. We should not fear for the tree, John. It is not alone but always remains with us in memory. The tree represents our life, John, the peace that erodes everything in due time. Look, John, I have brought these leaves for you. Let us keep them in our silences, in our bed of stone and moss. In the shadows of the night, John, I have brought you these crowns of fire.

amherst

In leaf season, the time of shadows, I approach Amherst along winding roads. Severity does not exist. Arriving in Amherst is like entering history without urgency, in the certainty that true understanding requires its own pauses. Perhaps that is how Emily Dickinson imagined her moments, devoid of past or future. The only possible moment—now—does not seek pertinence beyond the vocation of assembling words.

In leaf season I assemble and disassemble books, small gestures of unspoken lives. And between incidental silence and speech, Emily appears, naming fragrances in the garden of her own invention. Mysterious Emily, forger of regular habits, living every day in the same place, not in seclusion but rather inside herself, imagining her own way of speaking and knowing.

No one imagines her to be a traveler. Amherst is her beacon, her anchor and speech. And yet she travels. Her hands are alphabets of words and stars, and her feet trace the footsteps of the dead. Birds, fireflies, and words build their nests in her house.

After so many journeys I return to Emily to study her words. I long to return to immovable times, when alliances were braided in a room, in a poem, or on an autumn leaf.

I learn that the world is in my own hands, in Emily's hands. When Emily glances towards the street and says that she loves the afternoon light and needs only the company of fireflies, the source of her permanence is a perpetual journey along the roots of the sun.

homeward

That journey through the dominion of words took on the persistence of memory. Writing meant searching for the instant, the present, the precise breath with which to speak, imagine, or feel. My hands were like roads, steppes, and miraculous stones that emanated an interior light from deep within while my pen rested upon wood, stone, or words. I did not leave my orchard, my secret garden, preferring to stay within the confines of the fragile walls I had constructed like poems. There I imagined familiar voices and others not yet heard. More than the journey, my vocation was the words about the journey, the desire to spread myself across the table, across history. And the words sprouted like enigmas, intense passion, or secret desires. More than anything else, they were images floating above the caress of the grass.

I wrote as if intoxicated, in the same way that I contemplated cities I had never seen. I did not search for cartographic order or a compass, only a pencil. I wrote in order to know happiness and the astonishment of this journey, always homeward.

york, maine

The fog arrives upon the landscape like a sovereign aware of her own place in history and legend, owner of the sea and its privileged horizons. At first she is a delicate dancer, opening a path via the most fertile of promises. Then she begins to embroider the roads. She descends along the coastline and cliffs and settles on the shoulders of those who love her.

On the coast of Maine I learn the vicissitudes of fog, her weavings and shadows. The apprenticeship consists of knowing how to stop, return to plenitude, and relax among the horizon's edges.

The sea receives the fog as a hostess awaiting an unannounced guest.

The fog descends upon the houses. I treasure her memories and clear gazes amid the enigma of this darkness. I surround myself with the elongated sleep of vigilance.

The fog covers the horizon, and it is impossible to decipher the precise spot where we inhabit ourselves. And yet, do we see the valleys, rivers, and the perpetual motion of the waves she hides?

Someone surprised by fog is fortunate because he or she discovers the attire, the scratched and oblique light of the eternal horizon, and the beginning of memory, which is the first journey. On the coast of York it is necessary to be light, to move carefully among the stones as if they were small signs or ships that have lost their way. We must allow the fog to grab us by the waists and sweep us into the clear darkness of the pine groves, entering the forest without hostility. We must be subtle, like a shaft of light or a mirage along the road.

the fortune-teller

In York I have caught myself looking at the visitors, sizing
them up beyond gazes, beyond history. York's fortune-teller
has spent more than fifty years in her room of discoveries and
prophecies. Amid velvets, crystals, and the roar of summer
winds, she sits in a small armless chair, its plush upholstery
torn by chunky squalls and faded by the gravity of storms.
Nevertheless she seems to be the sovereign of this town of
intrepid summer folk. She is from Egypt but does not remember when she left there and cannot say whether she hails from
Alexandria or Cairo. In York she is a permanent fixture, like
a subjugating force deciding the fate of poor and rich tourists
alike and of the young who encounter desire for the first time
along the edges of this coast.

She does not beckon or request, she is simply there, like
lighthouses in the most remote regions. Our hands are like
that. Our palms, the shapes of our voice and of our silences,
open up to her.

I draw near. It is summer, and life is less weighty, time is
measured in light, a hand is a chrysalis of the sun. She waits
for me to give her my hand. She says I must first make an offering to the sea and then fully extend my hand, no twitching,
let everything and nothing fit there. That is the meaning of
luck, she tells me. That is the meaning of faith.

Along the beaches of York, when summer announces itself
with confidence, I return to the fortune-teller. I like to see
her. It is as if the entire town were waiting for her even though

she has never left, even though she is anchored to every season, a statue that feels like a voice in the night.

beach house

There it stood as if emerged from a watery dream or a snail gone astray. On the vertiginous sand I saw it, even smaller than when I last left, the trees but saplings, the chimney curved as if fleeing the forest, the owls.

Calypso dreams have claimed its sea color, and like an old woman it seems to shrink from sunlight's cracks. I sensed it waited for me, and in the doorway where once I stood firmly, the wood now rested in my hands. I entered and managed for an instant to imagine that nothing had moved: almond trees, hazelnuts, violet fauna, mysterious lizards once ravenous reptiles. This was my house, sweet and serene like a beginning. Here I enumerated words, played with them like beads on a priceless necklace. I learned to recognize the birds and not to venture out if the wind foretold other omens. I used to rest my head on its stone walls and feel the soothing solitude alongside the darkness, alongside the dawn, where each of my dreams offered possibilities, where I pretended to be a happy princess or a sensible woman.

This was my house. The doorway still displays the mezuzah with the Ten Commandments that determined my history. The house smells of pine and refuge. Here I reviewed the crevices of my soul, felt fulfilled by the melodious sadness of growing up. And when I left this house behind, I took some of its small stones and branches dancing on pyramids of smoke.

This is my house. It lives on in stone and memory. It waits for me, and I tell it things as when I was a child murmuring secrets into its moist walls. I am and I am not. I recognize myself among the shadows. Everything I am I owe to it, to its humbleness, because it was small and poor and I saw it as grandiose, because it embraced all the beggars and elegant ladies and knew how to celebrate with a loaf of bread shaped like love upon a table of golden wood.

My grandfather died in this house. He closed his eyes as he faced the sea. I know that he, too, loved its discretion and hidden forests, always out of reach as in a dream.

So much time has gone by since I last was here, and now I embrace it and fill it with my stories. A territory inhabited by exiles, a world of nothing but words, it is older than I. It lives, accepts the elements, the antiquity of its beams, cracked windows, and tiny lights that come on when scarce visitors salute it. Today I return to my house, and from the solitude we wear like a tired suit, I enter. My face is the history of time. The moist mirrors return my voice to me, and I, too, feel like the grass or mint.

I have come home. The ghosts have set the table, the bread is an offering of love. I fall asleep. My grandfather and lost ancestors have arrived, the light from its windows is splendid, and my eyes do not inquire: they celebrate, resting on the undulating fire, whistling and relaxed.

Today I have come home. You waited for me and I opened the latch. I placed my cheek against your walls.

the cliffs

Perhaps it was the sound of each name, melodies accentuating certain syllables, or my desire to recover that which I had once loved, rocky and unnamed horizons, their stories etched in stone. My children, husband, and I reached the coast of Maine and the villages along the cliffs. We loved the names—Ogunquit, Damariscotta, Friendship—and the people were like the silence that enveloped them or the mysterious woods that over time offered more beauty, wisdom, and clarity.

Here I found a house, or perhaps the forest found it. We live by letting life direct the flow, what must and must not happen. Here time decides which pilgrimages or momentary flights we will undertake, like the light pursuing the wind as it stoops to embrace the pines.

Here all appeared tranquil, a response to the peace at the heart of the restful forest. In the distance the sea kept watch over the trees, framed them, and allowed us to rest. The locals set sail but respect the mysteries of their domain. Here there are two kingdoms, the sea and the forest, water and wood. Both conjure adventure, yet the trees belong to the sea, from where they derive their wood. An imaginative navigator can see small oceans at midnight, coves shaped like horseshoes, a crown of trees within a circle of water.

Of all the places I have loved, have touched with my feet and hands, I love the coast of Maine and my house in Ogunquit because it is like others in which I have lived: vulnerable as if made of water, of pines aloft like sunbeams over the prairie. Here I feel and I let things happen to me. I plan nothing and know not the direction in which I will travel next. Time passes slowly and quickly. This is where I like to be because I remember everything with happiness.